Help! Save Me from My Broken Heart

Your Journey to Living and Loving Again

Adelai Brown

Adelai Brown

ISBN: 0692103546

ISBN-13: 978-0692103548

Library of Congress Control Number: 2018906397

DEDICATION

This book is dedicated to my husband, Kevin. Thank you for loving me to life and allowing me to be myself, whoever that may be at any given time

This book is also dedicated to the courageous souls willing to be vulnerable enough to do whatever it takes to be made whole.

Books by Adelai Brown

Anchored! Be Blessed! Daily Volume One

Help! Save Me from My Broken Heart:
Your Journey to Living and Loving Again

CONTENTS

ACKNOWLEDGMENTS

There are far too many people that helped me throughout the process of writing this book for me to name. Whether your impact seemed big or small, it was all major to me. It played a part in allowing me to create this amazing tool designed to support healing, enlightenment, authenticity, revitalization, and transformation in the lives of all those who read this book.

I want to acknowledge a few people who specifically blessed me during the book creation process.

Special thanks go to:

- ♥ LaVondilyn Watson for suggesting that I teach about a spiritual heart transplant. You challenged me to bring this product to life and I am forever thankful for it.
- ♥ Alisha Rose for being bold in Christ and urging me to write this book.
- ♥ Yolanda Gibbs, Adrienne "Peachy" Cox and Maria Manson, my Sister Girls, your unique gifts inspired and activated my gift. Thank you for pushing me to improve, even in unlikely places and spaces. I love you to life.
- ♥ Kat Ponds, my accountability, prayer, and writing partner through the entire writing process. I am thankful for your persistence and push. It made this experience better and I was able to complete the book in a timely manner.
- ♥ Rachel Langley for creating a beautiful, soul stirring book cover. It captured the beat of my heart and I know it will do the same for others. I appreciate your patience, skill and craft. Thanks for being my friend. (www.rachellangley.com)
- ♥ Kelly Bickel, Rachel Langley, Maria Manson, and Kat Ponds, my editing team. You all helped me to make my thoughts legible and understandable. I appreciate you.

♥ Susan Beach, my mother for being willing to heal along with me. This process has not been easy but it has been worth it. I am thankful for where we are now, and where we are going. I love you, Mommy.

♥ Aris Richardson, Twanna Ladson and Lorann Cook thank you for being sounding boards as well as complaint cushions. Your gentleness soothed me through some really tough times. I love y'all.

♥ Kevin Brown, my husband, and our four beautiful children: Akaris, Laniyah, Kevin Jr., and Kristopher. You all are the greatest inspiration behind this book. I want to heal and grow into a better woman because I have you all in my life. Thank you for being patient and supportive throughout the entire process of writing this book. God will reward your obedience and sacrifice. I love y'all.

CHAPTER *1*

I'm in Pain

Imagine sitting at home and your chest starts to get really tight. You know that you're tired from a long day's work, so you think to yourself, "Let me lie down and get some rest." You lie down and find yourself uncomfortable. "It must be indigestion from the quesadilla I had for lunch," is what you tell yourself as you head to the kitchen for a glass of water. As you drink the water, you notice you're getting hot and feeling weak. You are beginning to realize this is not normal and proceed to call your husband on the phone. Before he can answer, a sharp pain shoots through your heart and you realize you're probably having a heart attack. As he says "Hello" the phone falls to the ground, just before your body hits the floor. You hear what is going on, but you have no ability to respond... What are you going to do?

"He makes me sick!" I yelled angrily at the sky as I stormed outside. Frustration turned into rage and the default defense mechanism, my independence mantra, began to charge out of my mouth, "Oh yes, he must be mistaken. I don't know who he's playing with. I'm a strong black woman! I've been taking care of myself for a long time and I don't need anyone or anything (especially not a man), but God, to help me through! I don't need anyone!" I had been wounded and hurting for so long I didn't know what truly being at peace felt like, yet, I always convinced myself that I was okay. "I'll be okay. As long as I have God and my children, I can do ALL things through Christ who strengthens me!"

I was frustrated. Being absolutely convinced that I was right and my husband was wrong, I cried to God asking, "Why is my husband so difficult? Why can't he just do what husbands are supposed to do?!" With tears rolling down my face, I cried out, "I'm seeking You, so why won't he seek You with me?" This personal pity party spewed out of my mouth as I pleaded with God.

With a self-righteous attitude, I had foolishly convinced myself that my routine time spent with God was, in some way, VIP access to the Most High. I used my relationship with God and my acceptance of Christ to cover the pain of my broken heart versus acknowledging the pain and allowing it to heal. I seemed to have forgotten that salvation is free (For it is by grace you have been saved, through faith--and this is not from yourselves, it is the gift of God. Ephesians 2:8), but then again, when you're a person who doesn't feel worthy, like I was, it's hard to ever feel like you, or anything associated with you, is ever good enough. I was broken.

My brokenness was driving a wedge in my marriage and family relationships that I had yet to truly realize, but could no longer afford to be naive to. At this point in my marriage, two years in, I was just beginning to discern that the damage done to my heart, a product of the hidden hurts and burdens that I had been carrying since my youth, was hindering me from being able to wholeheartedly love my husband. This dysfunction prevented him from being able to completely love me because I was afraid to open my heart and truly receive his love. Even worse, this heartbreak didn't just plague my marriage; it also affected my relationship with my children, parents and my pursuit of fulfilling my purpose. The disdain that I had for myself, the negative self-image and the thoughts that I created about my life, were all a product of a broken heart that was projecting a negative narrative on the big screen of my life. This narrative was turning into a horror movie, with me as the star.

I was tired of going through this hurtful cycle. I was secretly diminishing. I was serving God, but my personal life - my family and desire to fulfill my purpose - seemed to be in more turmoil than the lives of those who didn't love the Lord nor did they have a desire to serve Him.

CHAPTER 2

WHY AM I SO BROKEN?

I wanted to know why my life was so difficult. How could my family get "fixed"? How could I get some relief? Something had to drastically change. I needed a new inner heart and I had to prepare myself to have it. I received a *Divine Heart Transplant (DHT)* and it changed my life.

I know that you may have heard of physical heart transplants being done on those who suffer from a defective, damaged and/or diseased cardiac organ in their bodies, but this heart transplant will help heal some of the hidden pains that only you and God can confront. It also allows you to make room for a more fulfilling and productive life. Many people think money is the answer to all of their problems. In my opinion, love and peace pave a path for one to be able to enjoy their resources. You must have faith in what's been placed inside of you before you can be successful with external gifts.

The DHT helps you to learn to embrace yourself. My hope is that you receive the same type of relief I received from this life enhancing procedure. I want even more for you to receive the renewed heart that God has for you. (I will give you a new heart and put a new spirit in you; I will remove from you your heart of stone and give you a heart of flesh. Ezekiel 26:36)

My divine heart was defective and I was in denial. It was weak and broken from the beginning of my life. It took me years of courage, and faith in Christ, to uncover and address the source and product of this brokenness. I know you may be wondering, "Why was she so broken?" I'm about to tell you why, but first, you have to make me, and yourself a promise. Promise me that you will take some time to truly think about what I am saying to you. Any thoughts that may arise of past hurts, future fears, or current discomforts, WRITE them down as you take this journey. Also, I want you to commit to writing down any thoughts of peace, joy, love, hope and expectation. When repairing a broken heart, you have to pay attention to all symptoms and signs. Every situation is teaching you more about yourself and giving you clues on how to live and love again, and for some, love for the very first time.

I believe in journaling, or chronicling your life so you can experience the cathartic peace of releasing and the gratification of being able to reflect on such an experience. Habakkuk 2 says "Write the vision, make it plain," and I firmly believe in this. You have to commit to being a student of life, or shall I say, a patient of the Master Surgeon, who will transplant your broken heart and make it anew. Students take notes. Yes, I am taking this journey with you, but this divine transplant is solely yours to undergo and conquer. I won't be able to make the sacrifices you'll make or confront your issues for you, but I will be praying for you and believing for you along the way.

I made a commitment to reach out to you by way of this book. I get joy in knowing your life is transforming with every page you turn and every step you take toward receiving your new heart. I'd love to hear about your progress and support you as you travel this journey. Join the Heart Support community on Facebook http://bit.ly/heartgroup. There are women just like you, in various stages of the DHT process - preparing, recovering and healing - and I know that you'll find support and sisterhood to reinforce and encourage you along the way. You can also follow me on YouTube at http://bit.ly/heartconnections and get updated teachings on the DHT process, and so much more. I want you to know that you are not alone. You'll need that reassurance along this journey to wholeness.

Brokenness begets brokenness

I had always struggled with a lack of self-worth. I beat myself up for not being good enough, smart enough, pretty enough, big enough, small enough, neat enough - I just could not get enough of anything. My heart had a void in it from my conception that robbed my life of years of fulfillment. I tried to fill it, trust me. I overachieved. I competed. I conformed. I rebelled. I did all of these things and nothing seemed to shift the negative image of myself that was painted on the canvas of my mind. Yes, I was celebrated. Yes, I was loved. Of course, I was supported, but for years that love and support fell through those cracks, the voids in my heart, that had weakened my capacity to truly love and be loved.

Can I be honest with you? My brokenness did not begin with my marriage. No, no way. This heartbreak that I speak of began when I was a little girl, just like a child being born with a heart defect. I had a heart defect, but it wasn't a physical defect in the heart that beat in my chest. This defect was in my soul. I absolutely believed that something was fundamentally wrong with me. That contaminating thought was weaved into the fabric of my personal identity. This debilitating lie emotionally damaged my self-image and was a precursor to the internal heart disease that plagued my life.

When you think about the idea of being saved from a broken heart, let's first think about what the word broken means. Broken means to be violently separated, damaged, weak, and/or infirmed. It can also be defined as not working properly, irregular, interrupted, and full of obstacles. Simply put, it's clear that there is a broad scope of brokenness and the many facets of life that it affects.

What does this mean for you?

A broken heart is a weak heart. Maybe you've experienced pure hell in your marriage or life altering issues with your children. Maybe you had a great childhood, however, under a microscope; it was plagued with hurts and offenses that rocked you to the core. You may want to send your children back to the God that blessed you with them, runaway or adopt a new extended family that appreciates and supports you. Brokenness shows up in many ways.

Be honest, you've probably said "I'm okay" so much you don't even think about how you truly feel when you're asked the question. You're not okay, and it's okay to finally admit it. Being transparent about where you are in life is probably one of the greatest challenges that you will face. Living and existing in a life with a broken heart truly limits one's ability to live authentically through vulnerability and transparency, and it also limits the ability to give and receive love and fulfillment.

How do you know if your heart is broken?

Let's think about this a little. Do you find yourself always giving more than you receive? Do you please and comfort others to the detriment of yourself? Have you completely had enough of your marriage and are ready to leave your husband? Do you secretly resent your children for reasons you often have trouble explaining or even admitting?

What about receiving help? Have you ever been so wounded by those seeming to lend a helping hand or assist that you would rather suffer without than to ask for their help, again? And, even worse, have you been experiencing health issues in your physical body that, if you'd be honest, can be traced back to the stress, pain and burdens that you've been carrying over the years? You've always been there for everyone else, now is the time for you to receive a divine heart examination and have a real assessment of where you are, internally, and prepare for your road to healing.

If you can relate to any of these examples, and others, you've probably built up a wall of defense that has undoubtedly prevented people from completely hurting you (or so you think). This wall of defense, the hardening of your heart, may have prevented people from hurting you, but it has also harmed you by preventing new love and healing into your heart. Self-preservation often creates self-inflicted wounds. This makes the old adage remain true--hurting people hurt people.

Those years of compounded pain have caused you to be doubtful about living your life to the fullest. The fear of being disappointed by others, yourself, and more importantly, God, causes you to "play safe" and limits your true expression of love and purpose.

Listen - your secret is safe with me. You don't have to be ashamed of the thoughts, or shall I say, symptoms, that you are currently experiencing. Thoughts and feelings of low self-esteem, depression, anger, rage, suicide, insecurity, jealousy, envy, and not being good enough are all debilitating. Because broken heartedness is sadly so common, many of us have experienced these pains but many aren't brave and courageous enough to admit it.

I know how it feels to question God, and to be downright angry with Him, when the trials of life seem to defeat you in every battle. My life was riddled with these thoughts and feelings, though I kept a smile on my face. That's the hypocritical life I lived when I questioned God many days. I couldn't understand why it seemed like I was being punished for seeking Him and trying to be a better person. The problem was, I had to realize I was already better and God was waiting for me to embrace that awareness. Needless to say, it took me undergoing my DHT to understand that God never left me-it was just my perspective that was distorted.

With that being said, let's review some guidelines, the "preoperative instructions", for you to follow as we go through this journey.

1. **Let go of the idea of who you think you are!** Let's be real, if you truly knew who you were, your heart wouldn't be broken and you wouldn't be reading this book. It's time for you to explore the being that is you, who God created to reign in the earth. An outdated self-identity only hinders present and future personal development.

2. **Embrace vulnerability as a strength and not a weakness.** Use your testimony to overcome past hurt and disappointments.

3. **Don't judge yourself.** The type of transformation you're about to undergo requires you to be honest, often brutally honest, with yourself. You can't afford to hide or pretend at this point in your life. Jesus can't heal what you won't confess.

4. **Mentally and emotionally dump.** Whether it's a journal or a composition notebook, always have something to jot your thoughts and ideas as you embark on this journey back to your God-given self.

CHAPTER 3

EXPOSING THE SHRINE OF PAIN

I've talked to hundreds, if not thousands of women who have been idolizing their pain and they don't even realize what is going on. Let me explain.

I was having a conversation with a good friend of mine and I came to this awareness. My friend is a wonderfully amazing woman of faith who loves the Lord and believes in His power. One day, we were talking about a hurtful situation in her life. She mentioned how her safe haven isn't available to anyone but her. What is her "safe haven, you ask? It's the emotional, spiritual and mental space that she retreats to inside of herself, when she's been hurt or violated. At the time, she was preparing to get married, and I was curious how she could have such an individualized mentality as she embarked upon such a sacrificial and interdependent union. Her candid reply touched me. She transparently said, "I am not willing to give up my safe haven. It's all mine. That's how I protect myself, and I am not willing to give that up. If I give it up, I won't have anything left to protect me."

Whew… Her honest truth stopped me in my tracks while enlightening my soul. I felt her pain because I too had a safe haven to run to, or so I thought. At that moment God revealed to us a startling truth. That safe haven, the dark space in our hearts where we retreated from pain and fear, as safe as it may have seemed, was actually a shrine of pain that we were worshipping. This emotional wasteland actually contributed to the negative outlook, mentality and perspectives that were preventing us from living our lives to the fullest potential. We were worshipping the pain and not the God who could heal that pain. Essentially, nursing dis-ease in our hearts.

This shrine wasn't a new occurrence that just magically appeared, oh no. It was fortified with years of trials, disappointments, heartache and violation that went improperly treated. Just like a disease not diagnosed and remedied in the natural body, the years of insecurity, hurt and pain had become my battle scars I was proud of having, even if they had infected my self-image and self-worth. I used to associate my identity with disappointment, lack and pain. I didn't expect to ever live a life free from the burden of having pain, so I never sought to truly release it. Why should I? Did it matter that much? Who would truly care?

What is worshipping the pain, you ask? Yes. When you hold on to the pain and pride yourself in being able to protect yourself from anyone or anything that can hurt you, and/or potentially help you, that is worshipping pain. If you can relate to this thought, and you too possess this space, you have more faith in the thought of being hurt again than you do in the promise of God blessing you. It's a tough truth that I had to accept. As much as I could justify the reasons for my internal armor, it didn't make it right for me to hold onto what happened.

My life was emotionally cluttered and it manifested in the relationships around me. I was moody with my husband and children, and I couldn't seem to find fulfillment in anything but work. At work, I thrived. I was able to give my all with no other expectations other than my performance. I found my value in my doing. At home, it seemed like the more I did, the less I saw progress. When I was at work, I'd focus my frustration on the work I needed to do, and I got the job done. There was progress, and there was a place that I could retreat to, and no one would really know. They wouldn't know that in work I had also found a physical space that mirrored the safe haven for my soul, one that I often retreated to.

God wants you to worship Him and not your pain. The pain infects and impairs us, which is what causes our hearts to break and stay broken. If you are going to be healed and thrive in the life that God has created you to live, you will have to let go of the pain that is burdening you and be vulnerable (yes, vulnerable--we'll talk more about that shortly) to the process that will transform you.

I know that you can't give your precious areas to just anyone, but God will allow you to have certain people that will be a safe space for you to unfold. God uses His people in the earth to bless each other. Have you been praying for God to bless you while subconsciously rejecting the messenger of blessings?

Think about it. You deserve to be free. If you want your husband to be real and honest, upfront and transparent, you too have to be willing to model the same behavior. If you want your friends to be supportive and trustworthy, you must also offer the same courtesy to those you consider your friends. What am I saying? The ability to love and live to the fullest will never come without the potential for pain, but we can't let that stop us. We must be willing to move forward, cry out for help when needed, and stand strong in the truth that you are NOT what you have been through.

Consider giving the Holy Spirit access to your safe haven. You'll be surprised at the type of cleanup and restoration work that will take place in your life. The truth is, if you're like me, you were tricked into believing that you can compartmentalize your life. Have you ever found yourself being one person at work, another at home, another at church, and yet another with your friends? That is a very exhausting existence that I once lived. It's very easy to live behind masks when feeling like you always have to protect yourself. When releasing your wounded spaces to God, you will find yourself living an authentic life that allows you to be yourself, no matter the environment.

The shrine truly isn't a safe place. As you journey to living and loving again, don't be afraid to confront your pain and trample your fears. It's time for the shrine to come down. The beauty of it all is that you don't have to do this all alone. There can be no areas of accepted darkness as you heal your heart. Such areas can become catalyst to heartbreak and heartache again. Don't hurt yourself unknowingly. Let the pain go. God is light and in Him there is no darkness (1 John 1:5). As the master surgeon, the Most High will begin His healing work. His love heals your pain. You know the pain I'm talking about. It's the pain you may have so deep-seated that it taints your heart, and you may not have even realized it is there. This pain prevents you from living a life that brings honor and glory to His name. His healing lifts you up to live a life that brings honor and glory to His name.

CHAPTER *4*

HURTING IN SILENCE

"I imagine one of the reasons people cling to their hates so stubbornly is because they sense, once hate is gone, they will be forced to deal with pain."
James Baldwin

Living with pain is a norm for millions of women, and it's not acceptable. For a very long time I thought my pain was normal because I never knew life without it. We have to be willing to confront the issues that hurt us most.

One of the telltale signs of heart disease is fatigue and loss of one's ability to operate at one's fullest capacity. Sufferers experience shortness of breath, swelling and loss of mobility. When the heart isn't pumping at the proper capacity blood doesn't efficiently flow throughout the body. When blood doesn't flow properly, necessary nutrients aren't able to properly nourish the body. Simply put, a sick heart prevents the rest of the body from being able to thrive. As a coach, I've encountered many women with heart disease of a divine nature. They have grown so accustomed to the dysfunction and pain in their lives that this divine illness goes undetected.

This thought process alarmed me. I am not a psychology expert; however I am a Heart Coach. I specialize in the area of coaching women to confront matters of the heart and live authentically on purpose. I love what I do because it brings my heart joy. I know how it feels to be in denial about the state of your internal affairs-your heart, emotions, and self-image. I used my relationship with Christ to mask the pain I was experiencing from the weight of carrying guilt, shame and unforgiveness for years. That burden infested my heart, and I couldn't heal. I was living below my capacity because my heart was dis-eased and operating at a limited capacity. I'm not talking about my physical heart, though that came into question at one point. The heart I speak of is spiritual. Housing my soul, it's the part of me that makes me-Me. It also embodies my thoughts, dreams, and even my prejudices.

How could it be? Like you, I went to church religiously, so I was current on my routine doctor checkups. I seemed compliant on the surface, but I was not completely honest with God at my weekly checkups. This lack of compliance was hindering my dis-ease from being detected and treated.

I wasn't paying attention to the symptoms. I had convinced myself that everything was okay, and it wasn't. After growing up with a tumultuous teenage experience, the battle wounds struck deeper than I realized. The side effects and undetected infections from these wounds plagued my twenties.

I was broken

I had such a heavy guard up through my roaring twenties I didn't realize the damage my heart had withstood. My heart had been hardening for years and I wasn't aware. I was spending time with God, reading my Bible, praying, fasting and participating in fellowship, but never truly communicating with Him about how I was honestly feeling. I was using Jesus to cover up instead of allowing HIs precious blood to set me free. I was angry at the fact that I was committed to Him, but I struggled financially. I did not like the fact that I could give everyone else advice in their relationships, but my own relationships continued to struggle. I despised my mother and father in my heart because I hadn't truly forgiven them. I just tolerated them, and that was not acceptable.

I felt like I couldn't help myself. I was hurting. My heart was broken. I went to church every Sunday carrying these burdens, and I carried them back home with me every time I left. This went on for years. And I know I am not the only one. I watch women work and serve in church faithfully, loving their families and church families. I have also watched them be mean and vindictive, cause confusion, and serve grudgingly for years. This is a heart issue. Many of us have been afraid to tell God how hurt, angry, disappointed and rejected we feel in this world called life. We are so accustomed to presenting this strong and fearless image of invincibility and it doesn't allow for vulnerability and transparency. The only way you can truly release your burdens is to disconnect from them. The only way your heart can be healed is to expose it.

I used to make excuses for my pain. Whether it was my bad attitude toward my husband or in my interactions with my daughter, I always had a justifiable reason for why I was acting inappropriately. My reason almost always revolved around some trauma I had experienced in my past.

If Kevin (my husband) didn't respond to me the way I desired for him to or perform in a way that I envisioned acceptable, I would revert back to my safe haven. The place that I thought was a retreat, refuge, and sanctuary from the pain was actually harboring toxicity and creating an infection in my heart. Sadly I couldn't see it. But Lord knows I felt the pain. I carried it with me every day of my life. It took my heart to begin to heal for me to realize the safe haven was not the Promised Land for my pain. I soon found out vulnerability, authenticity, and confrontation were the balm to heal those wounds.

The problem was I was afraid to do any of those things. As we take this journey, I want to start off by reminding you of this truth. The first part to solving a problem is admitting that a problem actually exists. That is half of the solution, or shall we say, the remedy to the problem. As a coach, for the past eleven years, I have encountered thousands of hardened women who were broken, hurting, and in utter denial about the pain they are carrying. Truth be told, I don't have to reference other women for examples of secret heartbreak. I can use myself as an example of what denial and a lack of vulnerability can do to your heart. It emotionally and physically depleted me and the quality of my life.

That way of thinking has to come to an end. Families are struggling, our world seems to be in an uproar, and no one seems to want to talk about the pain we're all experiencing. This journey is intended for you if you want to be helped. You know help is necessary and you can't go any further without the healing that is essential for you to be the best representation of yourself. Love yourself enough to commit to this process.

For years I carried disappointments and frustrations like a badge of honor. I thought it was honorable to delight in the fact that I would "take a licking and keep on ticking" or be able to "bounce back" from any low blow punch life threw my way. I had no idea how delicate my existence was. I wasn't designed to constantly stay in battle with life. The idea of brandishing strength and not appearing weak is deceitful. It is more comparable to a mental, emotional, spiritual, and physical blockade. I was trying to protect my heart by only allowing others in as much as I was willing risk getting hurt. I was protected in this space, but it would never be a place that would stimulate my healing. It was like I was isolating my heart in a padded prison cell.

I would never renounce my love and reverence for God, however, my inability to wholeheartedly rely on Him was making me weak. Though I read my Bible and was active in the church, I had no idea how weak my heart was due to my unwillingness to expose my "safe haven" to the only one who could rescue me from it. I had placed trust in my own independence, idolizing my own feeble strength. I was completely neglecting the power and benefits of the blood that Jesus shed for my healing. By His stripes we are healed (Isaiah 53:5).

Why am I telling you this? I want you to stop lying to yourself about how you really feel. If you have been violated, abused or mistreated, in anyway, now is the time to expose it. I know it has been very hard to do this in the past because others may have disappointed and let you down. I sincerely come to you asking for you to let go of that memory and begin to make new ones. I am not minimizing your experiences. You may have been bullied, disappointed, lied to and cheated on. That doesn't mean you deserve it, nor does it mean you have to continue to live that way. The DHT process is designed to help you release your old identity, while embracing a newer, truer identity in your God-given purpose.

Heart Check

Ponder these questions as we move forward. Journal your responses.

- ♥ Have you ever felt pressured to emotionally barricade yourself from those you love most? If so, why?(I want you to really think about this and honestly answer.)
- ♥ Have you ever limited your quality of life in an attempt to control the amount of pain you may experience?

When your heart is broken you're in a constant battle for your life. Your natural reaction to protect yourself from others trying to hurt you can easily harden your heart and affect your ability to truly love, and be loved. This form of self-preservation can easily morph into a form of idolatry of self, even if you don't realize it. We've been taught to be strong and fearless. That mentality is killing us slowly because it creates a lack of self-love and resistance to vulnerability.

Don't serve your pain by feeding your ego. Don't deny yourself the ability to heal because you're not willing to expose your wounds. If you're like me, you've found this safe haven is taking up too much space in your relationships. I was always frustrated with my husband, feeling like I needed more from him. I would write letters and have long conversations with him about how I needed him to love me more and show it to me. I needed him to be more emotionally involved. I was so unfulfilled; I even started throwing around the "D" word (divorce). That's a powerful word that should never be spoken in a God-ordained marriage. Pain will make you do and say some crazy things. This is why we have to get help.

I had cocooned myself into such a realm of self-protection and self-righteousness (pride), I didn't realize how delusional I was. It wasn't until I cried out to God one day and He stopped me in my tracks. I heard so clearly, "You want him to give so much of himself, but you're not willing to give all of you." It hit me like a ton of bricks. That was the moment I realized that my breakthrough was on the other end of my healing. I had to let all of my guards down in order to get what I wanted from my husband.

"I'm not sure I'm willing to do that," flowed out of my heart via my mouth as I came to this humbling realization. I mean, I was willing to serve God to no end, but I had yet to arrive at the idea of serving my husband in that way. That type of service requires vulnerability and unconditional love. I wasn't willing to give anymore of myself at that time. Truth is, I doubted if I even had the capacity to possess that type of love to give in the first place.

I excused my lack of commitment to this new thought process by telling myself that I wasn't mature enough at the time. Other women can live those stellar lives in service to God, their husbands, families and communities; however, I'm not one of them. At least, I thought I wasn't.

Why couldn't God fix Kevin and just let me be? Why did I have to give in? I would soon find out these answers, and many more-the answers to the mystery of why my life was so unfulfilled, even though I had Jesus.

This is one of the reasons why admitting that you're in pain is so important. When you admit that you have pain, God can help you deal with the source of your ailment, not just the symptoms. You deserve to live a life of freedom and abundance. God created you to thrive and live your life to fullest. Have your relationships, personal and professional, been mirroring the abundance Jesus died for you to have? If they haven't, I can assure you that the pain you've been keeping private is causing you public turmoil and dis-ease.

I was nervous and excited all at the same time. What would letting my guards down look like? What would it feel like? The thought of doing such a thing almost sent my heart into shock. I couldn't depend on myself any longer. I had to completely depend on God. Divorcing my husband was never the answer. If I left him, the pain of a broken heart would follow me and continue to consume my relationships. He wasn't the problem. It was me.

Can I be honest? I was angry with God for making me admit my pain and seek help. At the time, I was not woman enough to admit my anger. Having the background that I have, I was expecting God to make my life a little easier. I had a victim mentality. I felt as though someone owed me for all the pain I had been living with. If Jesus makes all things new, then let's just erase all of the years of hurt and shame I've experienced. In return, I'll take a perfect life with a perfect husband, perfect children and a perfect bank account. I deserved it, right? Hadn't I already struggled enough?

All of these thoughts raced through my mind as I embraced the revelation. The road to a purposeful life, complete with living and loving to the fullest, is paved with vulnerability, transparency and FAITH. The only vehicle that is equipped to travel this journey is authenticity. It's the only thing that can access the master surgeon's office and allow for him to evaluate the quality of your heart. It's also the only vehicle built strong enough to handle distractions and pitfalls you will encounter along the way. Being real with God, and yourself, makes room for the surgeon to work.

I didn't realize how broken I was until God reflected the spotlight I had been shining on Kevin, right back in my face. The power of that glare was life changing, to say the least. It was the moment I realized there was no value in holding on to the pain I had been harboring for so long in my heart.

CHAPTER 5

TRUST ISSUES

Yes, I said it. I said you have to trust, and I know you don't want to hear that. Your heart has been broken more times than you can count, and consequently, you have serious trust issues. Listen, I get it. You've been hurt before. I know it rocked you to your core. In order for you to get proper treatment and heal your broken heart, you must trust God, the Master Physician. Let me tell you a little bit about overcoming this deficit of trust.

I was struggling in my marriage because I told myself I would give my husband all of me; however, I did not truly understand what that meant at the core. Giving my husband all of me meant I had to trust him with all of me, and I was not willing to do that. I quickly realized that I had bitten off more than I wanted to chew. I was very guarded. I had stipulations that justified me holding on to pain, and the lack of trust I had for him. I was afraid to embrace the freedom of truly healing.

In my mind, he was the one with the problem. Honestly, most of the time, I truly thought that about everyone else- they were the problem. I had come to a place in life where I was the only person I truly trusted. I did not realize how much of my personality was built on a false sense of security in myself and a lukewarm faith in Christ. Let me explain.

My whole entire life I questioned if my father really loved me. He was absent from my life from age three until eight years old without one letter or phone call. He resurfaced in third grade via the telephone and packages through the mail, but I did not see my father again until I was fourteen years old. It was the summer before I entered the ninth grade. After this meeting, we saw each other a few times, until I wrote him a letter telling him how I felt growing up not having a father in my life. That letter severed our brittle relationship, again, and eventually we went back to being estranged.

Our estrangement ended briefly one fall afternoon. I was seventeen years old, and eight months pregnant with my oldest daughter, when I was involved in a very heated conversation with my father. After not speaking with him for about a year, he phoned, out of the blue, in an attempt to persuade me to convince my mother not to place him on child support for the last legal year of my childhood. If I complied with his request, he would help me and my unborn child get a car and a "head start" in life. If I didn't convince my mother, he would pay his support for the year, and I would never have to worry about him helping me and my baby ever again in life. I was furious.

I couldn't believe I was being pimped by my own father because he didn't want to pay child support. The man I had always wanted to love, accept, protect, and affirm me was basing the future of our relationship on a child support agreement between him and my mother. It broke my heart. That devastating moment shifted my whole perspective on love, life, parents, and men.

"If he won't love me, how can, or why would, anyone else want to? If your father doesn't want you, why would any other man?" are questions that ran through my head. Such heartbreaking thoughts for a little girl who soon found out she was living in a grown up world. I lashed out on him. I responded very rudely saying, "I asked her to put you on child support. You don't want to do anything else for me, so that's the least you can do. You have the money for it. You just don't want to take care of me. I will not ask her to drop this case."

He blew up. All of the years of being absent was staring him straight in the eyes. His little daughter wasn't sitting around waiting to please daddy anymore. She was fed up. We exchanged words. He responded the best way he knew how, with insults. The most piercing one came when he told me, "If I was in your life you wouldn't be pregnant right now. As matter of fact, your mom should've had an abortion instead of having you. I didn't want you anyway!"

I always sensed this inherent feeling of not being wanted. The day my father uttered those poisonous words to me every insecurity I had regarding him, and myself, was validated. I always questioned if he loved me, and that day I got my answer. He definitely did not love me, or at least that's what I assumed at the time.

My father doesn't want me.

Wow that statement really hurt. It hurt when it was said back then, but it gives me grace now because I can look back over my life and see how the divine heart transplant truly transformed me. It's humbling to imagine the changes that are possible when we release our pains to the One who saves. The pain I endured from my father contributed to my deep-seated issues with trusting people to help, support, and be there when I need them. I was such a lost and broken little girl, at that time. I already told you I was seventeen and pregnant, but I didn't tell you that I was a senior in high school living on my own. I was carrying the baby of a young man who had another girl pregnant, at the same time I was pregnant. Due to this toxic existence, I was experiencing complications with my pregnancy, and was put on bed rest. What a way for a girl to spend her last year in high school. What a way for a girl to enter into womanhood. This is a part of the reason why I convinced myself that I was the only person I could trust.

I felt like I was going to implode. People around me knew some of the facts about my life during this dark season, but no one knew about the dangerous conclusions I had reached to justify why my life was so toxic and chaotic. The only remedy I could think of was to toughen up. I convinced myself to get harder. I thought people were hurting me because I was being too nice, naive, and/or easily attainable. I hardened my heart in a desperate attempt to save myself. And it worked, or so I thought.

I had trust issues that prevented others from being able to bless me in various ways. I did not want to accept others support. I didn't want to be indebted to those who helped me. I was trying to stay in control by limiting how many people I had to repay, and/or defend myself against, because they helped me out in some way. Many of the people I felt should've cared for me didn't. I perceived this abandonment as the ultimate reason to only trust myself, and God when I chose to let Him in. I was young and wounded. Little did I know, my inability to trust others would negatively impact my future marriage, family, and professional relationships.

My trust issues were causing problems in my relationship with my husband, and more importantly, in my relationship with God. I did not trust God enough. My heart was too sick. I knew I needed help. How could I trust anyone else if I struggled with trusting God? I knew God was sovereign, yet I could not understand why He had allowed me to experience the pain, rejection and disappointments I had encountered.

My relationship with my husband was affected because I wouldn't get out of his way. I presented myself as very supportive, and I was, but I was also very independent and outright disrespectful when it came to me doing what I wanted to do. I felt like I couldn't trust him either. If I couldn't trust my mom or dad, how could I trust my husband, the next person obligated to take care of me?

Trust issues are heart issues

You may have been hurt or abused. The mean girls in school may have teased you about your complexion or acne problems, or you may have experienced abandonment from parents, like I did. You may have been touched inappropriately as a little girl, and it altered your ability to trust certain people for the rest of your life. Either way, this DHT will change your heart and allow you to explore trusting again - even when someone has hurt you to the core. I am a living witness, trusting others is possible.

Your joy and peace are important. Be open to allowing Christ to do this work in you - removing your heart of stone and giving you a heart of flesh - that you may have joy and peace, whether in times of blessing or times of trials and suffering. As you go through this process of uncovering all your heart issues, be open to getting to know yourself, the person God created you to be.

Your spirit, mind and body need you to invest in your healing - not just for your good, but for the good of the others, and most importantly, for the glory of God. Being afraid to trust Him and others is one of the most common ways to clog and harden your heart, and send you into heart failure.

CHAPTER 6

LIVING WITH A HARDENED HEART

One of the causes of heart disease is amyloidosis. Amyloids are natural proteins created by your body. When faced with dysfunction and trauma in organs, amyloids can calcify causing the organ to harden. This hardening causes soft tissue in organs to become like bone and, consequently, they aren't able to work properly. The calcification builds up over time and causes sufferers to eventually need a new organ in the areas affected.

As I think about the pain I've faced over my lifetime, I realize this process is what happened to my soul. There was no big situation that took place which just broke my heart; instead, my heart failure was caused over time. The long term build up I experienced reminds me of amyloidosis. This hardness represents a constant encounter with pain.

My dad's actions hurt me to the core. You have to be willing to acknowledge the issues that have hardened your heart. Some you've accepted as true, others you struggle with the validity of in your life. All I am saying is - stop denying the hardness you feel. It's evident in the way you live your life. How you show and express affection and interact with others who've mistreated you in some way are tell-tale signs about the texture of your heart.

I want to reiterate the fact that I am no expert in regards to the heart organ, nor do I claim to be. However, I do know when it comes to the spiritual heart; the divine essence within you, hardening is never a good thing. Jesus didn't die for you to stiffen in response to your pain, disappointment and rejection.

35

His blood is intended to make you more flexible, malleable, and useful. His blood gives you life. He doesn't take life away. Jesus is gentle. He was hurt and abused while never mumbling a single word. It was not because of His mistakes that He suffered the terrible death on the cross (Isaiah 53). He died for you, me, and the world. He conquered on the cross the hurt and pain He knew we would inevitably experience.

What He did for us is pretty amazing. That's true love. He did that for us. That's the donor heart you receive through this process. You have nothing to fear, except yourself. Your attitude and mindset as you travel through this journey will impact your success rate. Embracing the truth is one of the anchors that builds your trust in God, the Master Surgeon, and Jesus the Christ, the ultimate donor.

The issue of not receiving

If you are like me, you've struggled with being able to receive from others. Yes, you. You can freely give to others, but when it comes to receiving, you struggle in that area. That's a heart issue called pride. I hear you, "Pride, really, Adelai? I love helping others and I don't look for anything in return." That is what most of my clients have said in response to my allegation. Upon further investigation we often come to realize that there are self-defense mechanisms put in place, though subtle, that hint at the pride that prevents us from receiving.

I am explaining this to you because you have to prepare your mind, heart, and body for this major transplant. This shift will jumpstart your life and make for provisions along your journey of learning to live and love again. Pride prevents restoration because it halts forward progress. You can't truly connect with anyone or anything when you're emotionally armored and restricted. What you have to understand is your Master Surgeon knows what's best. Pride tells you that you have to protect yourself. Trust in God allows you the freedom to rest in Him and not have to always figure everything out.

I'll tell you what this looked like for me. As I began to invite Christ into my situation, I began to trust Him more. Trust in Him allowed me to revisit the trauma I had experienced in my youth. It helped me not to dwell in the pain, but take a different perspective from the situation. I realized that I was justified in my attitude of disgust toward my father, however it didn't make my attitude right. I was equipped with the tools to forgive him. Was I going to use them? The connection to Christ assured me that everything would eventually heal and come together, but I had to submit to the process. This process is very simple, but not easy.

Pride prevents connection. To connect is to bring together to establish a link or line of communication. This embodies the foundation of your divine heart transplant. It's hard to wholeheartedly connect with others, especially spouses and children, when your primary focus is self-preservation. You have to allow yourself room for change, and often that means making room to connect with others so that you can embrace a new perspective on life.

Mistaken Identity

You are NOT what you've been through! I have to reiterate this fact as we move forward. Many women refuse to seek help for fear of losing themselves. Losing themselves, you ask? Yes, a shift in identity takes place when you start to admit and address pain. This shift takes place because much of our present identity is rooted in past experiences. When you begin to declutter your past of unresolved pain and heartache, you'll find out you are more than you thought you were, and have potential to be greater than you ever thought you could be.

As you get to know yourself, don't fret when your life begins to get awkward. I don't want you to put this book down, refrain from journaling, or participating in any other form of healing when this process starts to get difficult for you. It takes time to get adjusted to this type of change. Awkwardness and discomfort are often signs that you're on the right track.

You are not your pain. It took me years to embrace this absolute truth. You are a delicate vessel. God created you to serve and love, but never to carry unnecessary burdens. I want you to consider getting the help, and I'm not talking about the help you get from friends or family. In order to heal the type of pain you've been carrying in your heart, you have to visit The Heart Specialist. Thankfully, this Specialist, unlike most cardiologists, always has available appointments and He never loses a patient. You have to commit to this transplant process, despite the inevitable challenges that will arise.

You may have identified with poverty, abuse, neglect and lack, at some point in your life, but that was never who you were. Healing your brokenness allows for you to adopt a new identity. Whether you undergo divine bypass procedures, or you obtain a new heart, your new identity is founded in Jesus. You will never have to worry about identity theft again.

Heart Check

As we move forward, take some time to reflect. Here are a few questions to ask yourself along this healing process. Journal your responses.

- ♥ What is your biggest fear in life?
- ♥ What is your biggest challenge in most of your relationships?
- ♥ How do you respond when your feelings have been hurt? Is this response productive?
- ♥ What do you want most in your life?

Spend some quiet time pondering these questions. You have to get in the habit of reflecting and getting to truly know yourself. I know you are great at researching others, but this journey demands that you not only get to know yourself, you must also begin to love and trust yourself. How can you trust yourself, if you don't even know who you are and why you do the things you do?

Now that you have reached a point where you can admit you're in pain, it's time to schedule your appointment with the Master Physician. I know you may be experiencing some anxiety when thinking about going to the doctor. Don't worry, we'll attack those trust issues in the next chapter. You have got to see this doctor, girl. He's about to change your life. For real, for real!

CHAPTER 7

MAKING YOUR APPOINTMENT

*"WE CAN LOOK FOR ALL THE MIRACLES WE WANT IN SCIENCE,
BUT I'LL TELL YOU WHAT THE GREATEST MIRACLE OF ALL IS,
IT'S THE TRANSFORMATION OF YOUR HEART UNDER THE POWER
OF GOD."*
DR. RAVI ZACHARIAS

You may be accustomed to visiting the doctor annually to receive a physical, but this appointment you're about to make is not routine in nature. You know that something is wrong in your life and this acute problem needs to be addressed. As you prepare to make an appointment with the Master Surgeon, keep in mind that His appointments are always open, you just have to be willing to set the appointment, and show up at your appointed time.

Identity Verification
I worked in medical facilities for over ten years. I loved working with patients, their families, and other health professionals to ensure that our patients received the best possible care. One of the most important pieces of information required to guarantee that a patient receives the proper care is personal demographic information. Who are you? If we, being the professionals who care for you, don't have your proper information, we can't offer you adequate care. The same goes for God, your Master Surgeon. He needs you to present Him with the proper information. Yes. He is all knowing and all

powerful, but a broken and contrite spirit He will not despise (Psalm 51:17). You are sick and now is not the time to try and commit identity fraud with the master of the universe. Be honest about who you are, even if you don't quite know who that is, at this time.

A part of exposing yourself to healing involves detaching yourself from lies about who you currently think you are. When you understand that you are a triune being- spirit, body, soul- then you can better understand who you truly are and what your purpose here on earth really is. Many women only view themselves from a physical standpoint. The pressures of this world have convinced them to invest all of their energy and resources into what people can physically see about them, often neglecting the very essence of their being, hence, going into heart failure. I don't care how pretty, sexy, and voluptuous you are. None of those attributes can protect you from the pains of a broken heart.

Let's take a little time to explore what your Divine heart really is.

What is Your Divine Heart?

My chest is hurting. My heart is hurting. I don't know what to do. I need to go to the hospital...

That is a common complaint of many who suffer heart disease. Let me be clear, I am not, nor do I claim to be a cardiac expert of the anatomy and functions of the heart, as it pertains to being a vital organ in the body. (Side note: I did get an A+ on my heart test in anatomy and physiology. LOL.)

I only reference the physical heart to parallel the importance of your internal divine heart in your existence here on earth.

Who are you?

As human beings we are made of three parts-body, spirit, soul-in the image of our Triune God who is made up of the Father, Son, and Holy Spirit.

The Body

Your body is the physical, tangible part of who you are. It encompasses the "flesh" that you often hear Christians speak of, and it is the hardest part of our anatomy to tame. Our physical body can be compared to a real life costume, or covering if you will, to envelope who we are at the core.

You are not your body--however, your body is a part of the whole of who you are. The body makes you aware of the physical environment around you. It reacts to your five senses. Many people are mistakenly under the impression that life only exists in the realm of what we can sense. The ability to taste, smell, touch, see and hear are all sensory mechanisms, possessed within our bodies, that allow us to examine and interpret life on an individual basis.

The body is the vehicle that allows us to physically move about and do God's work in the earth. This truth supports the importance of caring for your body. Discipline yourself so that you can maintain a healthy temple. Eating healthy, drinking plenty of water, getting lots of exercise and minimizing your stress levels are all ways to maintain a healthy body. A healthy body is better prepared to carry out the will of God to the full.

The Spirit

Your spirit is essentially what makes you, you. It is mankind's consciousness and awareness of God within self. This is an intangible part of your being that brings you to life. It is the offspring from God that He used to animate His existence in your body. Your spirit is Holy and wholesome. When someone dies, their spirit leaves their body and returns to God. It can be compared to universal DNA.

Just as your DNA chains tell the story of your earthly genealogy, and assures you of who your parents are, the very fact that you are alive and breathing is proof that you are the creation of God, from His very own bloodline.

Your spirit is the breath of God breathing life into you. It is in constant communication with the heavenly Father, its divine source. This is the "God" in you.

This is how we truly worship and commune with God. When you hear God with your inner ear, and feel His warmth moving through your body, some call it intuition, but it's actually your spirit delivering you a message from the Most High. Your spirit is your divine foundation that keeps you in constant contact with our Heavenly Father.

The spirit is communicating when you hear people speak in tongues. The warning signs that flash across the screen of your mind intending to prevent you from hurting and harming yourself, premonitions, if you will, are all a product of your spirit communicating with and through you.

The Soul (The Heart of Mankind)

The soul, also considered the heart, is the third part of your existence. It is an intangible portion of your being. Embodying the human will, intellect, and emotions, the soul is your ability to communicate with yourself, God and the environment around you.

Your personality, character, and logic are all compartments. The affections you delight in and the pestilence you may despise are all rooted in your soul, the heart of who you are. Just as the physical heart is the center of circulation for your body, your soul is the core of who you are, what you were, and all you can ever be.

Housing your desires, excitements, hurts and pains, your soul is the portion of you that thinks and reasons. Eve was using her ability to reason when she chose to eat the forbidden fruit in Eden. The soul is the place that was corrupted when she made that decision. God judges us by the quality of our hearts, or shall I say, the state of our souls.

Your soul is your divine heart, the core of your identity. Often confused with the Spirit, this is where we communicate within. This also the conduit used by the Holy Spirit to channel information from us to God, and from Him to us. A surrendered heart yields to the spirit of God within. A rebellious heart is driven by the five senses and ego. You protect yourself here. You allow yourself to love and live out loud in your soul. You also guard yourself and hold grudges here.

This is where we hide the symptoms of a broken heart and begin to uncover the pain. This is the place that spends eternity in heaven or hell. This is the part of you that is born again, and made anew, when you accept Jesus the Christ as your savior. This is part of you that will be surrendering to the master surgeon as He performs your Divine Heart Transplant.

Heart Check

You may feel a nudge in your heart to draw closer to Christ. If so, pray this simple prayer, and allow the Holy Spirit to move in your life.

"Lord Jesus, I love you. I thank you for saving me. Come into my heart and renew my mind. Protect me from myself so I may live more like you. Help me to be the person You died for me to be. I thank you in advance for answering my prayer. In Jesus precious name, Amen."

CHAPTER *8*

THE INITIAL CONSULTATION

When your heart is weak you have to go to the physician. If you are like me, you have tried to do everything you can to self-medicate your symptoms. That works for a while but there will come a time you will not be able to deny the pain.

I know going to the doctor is often a very terrifying experience. It causes anxiety and brings about reservations. Just the thought of attending an appointment can make a patient sick in and of itself. I worked in healthcare for over 10 years. I encountered hundreds of patients who furthered their sickness by their thoughts about the doctor. My experience also caused me to be a difficult patient. I knew so much about myself I thought I had my healthcare under control. I was pushed to the brink of destruction, more than one time. I had to make my way to the doctor, or shall I say, He made His way to me. It is definitely safe to say this physician makes house calls. In a day and time when finding good bedside manner is like finding a diamond in the rough, you can rest assured knowing God, the master physician, has an ease that gives you peace that surpasses all understanding.

Let me be very clear, you can NOT figure out your problem and heal yourself. You don't need eight years of medical school to heal a broken heart, however you absolutely need Jesus. He's the key to total transformation. My first real life encounter with the Master Physician made me realize how real Jesus is and how much I need Him. I was at the lowest point in my life I can ever remember.

After escaping a toxic relationship and abruptly realizing some close friends were not invested in our friendship the way I was, I was ready to give up on life. I was a twenty-year-old single mother struggling to make ends meet. My mother was on my list of adversaries at this time, as well. She and I had gotten into an altercation that left us not speaking and me with two black eyes.

I was so tired and so broken.

The burden of failure was so heavy I couldn't bear it. I was too prideful to ask for help, to let someone on the outside know how much I was really struggling and the emotional anguish I felt. I felt like a failure as a mother and a woman. I was financially depleted and mentally spent. I questioned the value of my life and the role I played in the world around me. I wanted out of the pain even if it meant out of life. I was all alone one day and something strangely blessed happened.

My life was pitiful. My thought process was contaminated. I believed I was worthless and did not have a valid purpose for being on earth. I paced the floor of my townhome trying to figure out who I could give my beautiful three year old daughter to because I surely did not deserve her. She had so much potential and did not need to be contaminated by a broken mother, like I had experienced. So I picked up the phone and started to call trusted family members and make my plea for someone to save my child from me. Every time I went to dial a phone number, it was like I hit a brick wall. I was internally reminded that this particular person truly could not help. I felt helpless.

In my despair I began to cry profusely. I was broken and I could not hold it in anymore. I felt my mental capacity slowly slipping away. I truly thought I was losing my mind. Neither my mom, my dad, nor my angel on earth, my Grandmother, could save me. I was lost. I was slipping into the darkness of my despair. And then, something amazing started to happen. The more I cried, the more I felt a sense on warmth and security rising up on the inside of me. It was as if this presence was melting my heart of stone and ice. I started to think to myself, "What is this? What's happening?", and almost simultaneously, I heard a response, but it wasn't audible. The soft whisper said "Jesus" and I cried even more. But now they were tears of joy and relief, utter and complete freedom.

Words truly cannot explain the feeling I experienced on that day. Jesus heard my cry and came to my rescue, right in the middle of my mess. Funny thing is, I never cried out to Jesus specifically, I just cried. I had been so disappointed by church and God, I honestly believed He was angry with me and the circumstances of my life were a direct response to that anger. When Jesus visited me that afternoon in my living room, I knew that He was all He claimed to be. I knew that my life would never be the same from that day on. And it wasn't...

The Diagnosis

The heart, a hollow muscular organ located in the chest of the human body, is about the size of a human fist (in proportion to the fist of the individual), and is the central hub for blood to be transported throughout our bodies. The heart is responsible for giving and receiving blood from the lungs to the rest of the body, and ultimately assuring that each body part, and function, is nourished with oxygen rich blood. Needless to say, our hearts play a major role in our existence so heart health-spiritually, emotionally, and physically-is of the utmost importance. We have to care for our core.

When the heart is broken, or isn't functioning properly, every other part of the body is subject to limited capacity for operation or failure. Heart disease is the number one killer of women in the United States; annually, one out of every four women will die from heart disease-related complications. And the scariest thing of it all: this heart disease is often a silent killer.

Just as in the cases of physical heart disease, many women are slowly dying from the epidemic of spiritual heart disease. Yes! Just as the malfunctions and dysfunctions of the anatomical heart usually increase and intensify over time, the ailments of your spiritual heart, the core of your being, are life-altering and purpose-threatening. These ailments are the result of years of hurt, pain, and neglect that went unaddressed, and subsequently, untreated.

Well, the Heart Coach ™ is here, working as 1st assistant to the Master Surgeon, God Heavenly Father, and it's time for you to undergo your spiritual heart transplant. It's time for you to release that old heart of bruises, baggage, and brokenness to receive a new heart that will expose and introduce you to a new life with the capacity to live and love again. It's an intimidating procedure, so prepare accordingly for the journey. This journey requires much sacrifice, but I am more than certain that you can do it. Don't doubt the Spirit of God inside of you. Your pain had a purpose, and now it's time for you to prioritize.

If I can be honest with you, my dysfunction didn't originate in my marriage. Instead, it was rooted in years of feeling inadequate and fundamentally distorted. Many people thought that I had it all together--I was loved by mother and nurtured by my family. So why did I think so negatively of myself? If this question crossed your mind, believe me, it had been at the forefront of my mind for years. That is a big part of the reason why I sought God for a spiritual heart transplant, and I am supporting you to do the same.

Honestly, there were many factors that were attributed to my heartache, but I'll only elaborate on a few.

Insecurity
I had daddy issues.

According to the US census bureau, in 2016, an estimated 8.5 million children were growing up in a home with a single mother. That is a startling number. I know that many children and adults have experienced this empty phenomenon, but that doesn't minimize, nor can it rationalize, the pain that growing up without a father creates. It's debilitating. Even if you grew up with your father there, but he wasn't mentally or emotionally available, you probably grew up seeking affection and attention from someone else in an attempt to satisfy the voids your dad did not fill. This is the debilitating reality for millions of children. For me, it was like growing up looking at a mirror that revealed only half of who I was, and only a silhouette of the elusive other half, the side that consisted of unanswered questions regarding the sower of the seed that created me. Not knowing my father, and not having a relationship with him for most of my youth, seduced me into believing that I was worthless and just not good enough. I reasoned with myself that if I was good enough, my father would have wanted to show up, support me, and prayerfully, love me.

That sad song played on repeat in my head for most of my youth and early adult life. The tune emitted a frequency that hardened my heart and thus began to weaken it, and ultimately weaken me. But I thought I was strong, I really did. I had convinced myself and others that I wasn't fazed by the lack of paternal presence and influence in my life. It broke my heart that I didn't have my Daddy with me. It hurt even more trying to convince myself, and others, that it didn't bother me.

I said things like, "I was raised by a strong black woman! We don't need men to survive! All I need is Jesus." Boy oh boy was that a damaging lie. The truth is, all I need is Jesus, but the lie was that I didn't need a man.

I needed a man. I needed to be loved. My vision was distorted from the unresolved pain I was holding on to. I had convinced myself that I could trust in the confidence I placed in myself. My independence was an idol causing problems in my life. Every relationship that I experienced reminded me of that truth. Jesus truly sacrificed His heart for us, so all we need is Him, BUT, He died so that we can use the love He gives us to share with and expose it to others. A broken heart caused me to give and receive love at a limited capacity.

Broken-Heart Syndrome

The truth about heartbreak is that it can cause a real life heart condition called *Takotsubo Cardiomyopathy*, otherwise known as Broken-Heart Syndrome. Yes. The stress, trauma, and pain you have been experiencing in life can adversely affect your heart in a way that can cause people to experience symptoms that mirror those of a myocardial infarction, also known as a heart attack.

Broken-Heart Syndrome is the consequence of extreme physical and emotional stress. It is more commonly found in older women, than men, and is often brought on by extraneous life experiences. Situations such as domestic violence, a bad breakup, loss of a loved one, receiving a terrible medical diagnosis, and/or extreme fear can all possibly contribute to the onset of this peculiar ailment.

Your body physiologically reacts to the thoughts you think, and environmental circumstances you face on a daily basis. This is powerfully important for you to understand. In Broken-Heart Syndrome, the hormones that the body releases when we experience some of the above named stressors, and more, literally adversely impact the natural functions of the heart, decreasing its ability to properly pump blood to the body. During this onset of broken-heart syndrome, there is usually no blockage present in the coronary arteries, like those found in most heart attack cases. The symptoms of broken-heart syndrome are acute - they usually last for only a month when properly treated by a physician-and often leave no long-term damage done to the heart.

I want you to remember this in your personal life. You may have endured extreme hardship - mentally, physically, and emotionally - and you feel like giving up. Know that you can overcome your pain. Your feelings are valid and real. Allow your soul to heal. Your heart doesn't have to suffer anymore.

Heart Check

Think about a situation in your life that hurt you long ago. Honestly answer these questions by journaling your response.

♥ Have you truly confronted and healed from it?

- ♥ Have you become accustomed to limping around in life, emotionally afraid to truly show and receive love and affection?
- ♥ Have you been paralyzed by your pain?
- ♥ Are you willing to release your paralysis and pain to be free?
- ♥ If you say that you've released it, how do you truly know?

The spiritual/divine heart, the central most innermost part of your being, is the place that God visits and evaluates. I was always trying to present myself the best way I knew how to others, however, I did not realize how vain this focus is. I wanted to be perceived a certain way, but I did not make nearly enough effort into making sure my heart was in order. I read and knew the scriptures, and I had frequent emotional experiences with God. My heart was right, right? I didn't need to work on me. It was those other people who needed Jesus. Not me. At the same time, I mastered in diagnosing my husband's "ailments." I had begun to believe I had the ability to judge his ways and his reasons for doing the things he did. I was being very self-righteous toward him, all the while disguising it as deep concern. Self-righteousness was a bandage that covered up the infection of insecurity that ruled my self-image. I needed a new heart and I didn't even know. It was time for some divine intervention.

CHAPTER 9

THE FIRST SURGERY

Undergoing the Divine Heart Transplant (DHT) is the way to overcome a broken heart. You may always see or feel the scars, but you don't have to feel the pain forever. I realized this fact at a pivotal moment in my life. This fact is what makes Ezekiel 36:26 such a refreshing truth for me, "I will give you a new heart and put a new spirit in you; I will remove from you your heart of stone and give you a heart of flesh." I questioned if I could be healed of the toxicity of my past because the wounds it left were so deep that current circumstances seemed to continuously fall prey to the infection that my past had left in my heart.

I told you that I had issues. I truly don't believe that my issues were unique in orientation, but they were personal and painfully debilitating. I now understand why our world is in the state that it is in. I truly believe if more people knew they could be healed of the wounds that didn't cause physical bloodshed, we would see less hate, animosity, and backbiting in our world today. With women, especially, insecurity and pain often morph into envy and jealousy. This behavior makes it almost impossible to connect with others. It's a sad epidemic that can be completely inoculated through the power and love of Jesus Christ.

Step One - Connection
The paralysis of heart disease causes many to need a new heart. This is true in the natural, but it is also true in the

spiritual realm, as well. Finding a donor, when the natural heart is failing, is often taxing and problematic. There are long waitlists filled with individuals buying time in life while awaiting a new heart, all the while knowing that someone will have to die in order for them to live. That's tough. The blessed thing is there are perks to receiving a DHT.

The first perk is that there is no waitlist for this life saving procedure. Aren't you glad for that? The second perk we'll discuss further.

A heart donor is usually an individual that has brain damage, or some type of death inducing trauma that causes them to die, but their organs are still able to be used to save the lives of others. These organs are harvested and used to keep others alive, but there is never a guarantee that the organ recipient's body will receive the organ. Unlike in the natural, a DHT is always available and the recipient is always able to receive the donor heart. How can I be so sure you ask? The donor is Jesus. He died a brutal death so that we can live an abundant life. This is so amazing. This a truth that you can stand on.

Heart transplants are very risky surgeries so many people question the success rate of the outcome. You won't have to worry about that through this transplant process. The Master Surgeon performing the surgery has never lost a patient, nor has this Donor ever had a heart rejected. All you have to do is prepare for this enriched perspective and sense of being to encapsulate you by way of a fully functioning heart that is equipped with the essentials needed to live and love again.

Haven't you experienced enough offense and rejection? Are you tired of being on guard and having to protect your heart and your passions?

I know the burdens you have been carrying have been tough. It takes much strategy and excellent execution to be both strong and assertive, yet gentle, loving and welcoming toward individuals you encounter on a daily basis, all the while feeling disregarded and overlooked. I get it. I was drawing closer to God and beginning to realize the majesty of Jesus the Christ. He came into my life in such a tumultuous season that I was smitten by the peace of God's word which was beginning to prepare and mold me for the change I was about to undergo. I knew God through my Grandma; however, I was getting ready to experience Him for myself.

Most of my adolescent life I thought I had done something to anger God, and that was why my life was so miserable. I blamed myself for the extra-long courtship I participated in with my husband (7 years) because I believed I wasn't truly good enough to be a wife. It was almost like he married me out of obligation. Let me be clear. That's not the way my husband treated me, but that was the way I perceived our relationship. That is one of the symptoms of a broken heart-always thinking the worst in a situation. Would I have admitted to you at that time, that I solely blamed myself for our relationship dysfunction? NO, but I can honestly reveal that now. I believed I was fundamentally wrong and my life was the product of that dysfunction.

The relationship I had with my mother did no justice to denying my thoughts of unworthiness. From the age of eleven to twenty-nine, my mother and I had a relationship that, nicely put, resembled oil and water. I love and admire my mother for being the strong and resilient woman she is, but to be honest, for years I resented her.

From the time I was a little girl I came to the conclusion I was never going to be able to please my mother. That unwavering burden was a major contributing factor to the feelings of unworthiness and shame I felt since I was about 9 years old. I felt if I couldn't make Mommy happy, how could I ever be genuinely accepted and pleasing to anyone or anything else? This negative mindset I possessed was emotionally and relationally debilitating.

If you don't think your mom loves you, how can you truly believe that anyone else does? I was a happy-go-lucky girl on the surface, but I had an intense internal battle brewing within. My heart was broken. I needed help.

The Virus of "They"

I always looked at others as better as or more noble than me. That was very frustrating. I was frustrated because I didn't feel like I could truly change my circumstance. Do you know how it feels to be in a crowd of people and question if they're looking at you or judging you in some way? I used to be so in tune to what "they" had to say that it would drown out my own voice, and worse, the voice of the Holy Spirit. The opinions of others were carrying more weight than the truths of God. Praise God for connection.

The fact that Jesus is your DHT donor makes for an ultimate connection. A re-connection needed to be established for me and my mother, but most of all, with me and Christ. A connection is defined as the action of linking one thing with another. In order for my broken heart to be healed, I needed to be connected to something greater than me. If you want your heart to heal, you have to be willing to link yourself to someone greater than you.

It's all right to acknowledge that you're weak in certain areas of your life. One of the major lessons that you will learn along this journey is that vulnerability is strength and not a weakness. I know you may believe or have been told otherwise, but the Bible confirms this truth in Revelations 12:11: And they have conquered him by the blood of the Lamb and by the word of their testimony, for they loved not their lives even unto death. It's going to be just fine. Don't get scared. I know the thought of letting your guard down is frightening, but you have to be willing to drop your defenses if you want to make new connections. Connections are vital, and you have to expose yourself if you want to make connections. In order to gain a new heart, you have to be willing to allow vulnerability to lead the way. It's also the best way to heal as you go through the process.

When you've been strong for so long, there will come a time that you'll realize your strength will wear out. This journey to living and loving again isn't about you being invincibly independent. Instead, it is about you allowing your spirit and soul to reconnect with the spirit of God and His perfect plan for your life. This stage of connection heavily involves you putting your faith in God's unchanging hand.

It is imperative that you remember God doesn't change! I want to reiterate this truth because undergoing a DHT will definitely drastically change YOU and the life you exist in. You will have to rely on your connection to God as you allow your old heart to become new. There will be situations you have to accept, but don't understand. Remember you are connected. There will be circumstances that uncover hurt that was buried deep down in your soul. Remember you are connected. You will want to stop the process when it requires more from you than you think that you can give. Just remember, you are connected.

Becoming familiar with your Donor

Getting to know your donor will aid you to better acquire His heart. He has so much goodness for you. This goodness includes release from shame, emancipation from regret, and a renewed sense of existence. When you commit to a divine heart transplant, divine connections transform your life from the core. You have to be willing to accept it.

His Character

Character is defined as the mental and moral qualities distinctive to an individual; the distinctive nature of something. I knew the character of everyone around me as I began my journey, so I thought that I had Jesus figured out. Boy was I wrong. If you're like me, you've been so hard on yourself internally, that it's hard to believe that Jesus would save you, and give you a new heart, when you don't feel like you have much collateral to bargain. That was my plight as I began the transplant process.

The hidden hurts I had developed into a deep sense of insecurity. I trained myself at a young age to gain validation through my works. Just like finding value at work, as long as I was doing and contributing, I found value. The problem I encountered early on was that Jesus did not require me to do or be anything or anyone but myself. This unconditional love took me a while to embrace. I could not understand how Christ could love me so much when my parents didn't even care. That was a serious battle for me to overcome, and I wrestled with that thought for years.

I had to get to know the character of Jesus. I heard what others said about Him, but I had to get to know Him for myself if I was going to survive. Psalm 27:10 says, "When my father and my mother forsake me, then the Lord will take me up." This was the passage that opened the door to this unconditional love. It seemed to me the Master Surgeon was so thorough, He had remedied my problem before it was ever created. I was trying to equate my natural familial relationship to my divine promises--and that was grossly incorrect.

I had to grow in the understanding that my heavenly Father has the capacity to infinitely love me on a level that my earthly parents could not even comprehend. Revelations like these are what make having a connection with your donor so important.

Flow

A defective heart isn't the only reason one may need a heart transplant. As I researched the anatomy of the heart and the causes of heart failure, I found there are two primary reasons for heart failure. One reason is a defective pump causing a lack of blood flow through the body. The second reason is an inefficient electrical current that is causing the heart not to function properly. This lack of electric flow prevents the heart from beating properly, consequently, hindering sufficient blood flow through the body.

These damaging symptoms of heart disease are sure signs that communication within the heart is faulty. The same concept applies in your divine heart. Certain circumstances you may have experienced, such as a strained or nonexistent parental relationship (maybe you never knew your mom or desired more affection from your dad) or abuse that went unnoticed and/or unaddressed (maybe you experienced molestation or rape that you were never protected from), may have created a poor connection. You may have even had a great upbringing, but struggled with self-acceptance and couldn't quite see the beauty in the mirror that God said He created you in. These situations have caused you to harden your heart and you may have emotionally shut down. You're probably operating in sleep mode, as you go through life with your loves and passions. Either side effect limits the ability to live and thrive in this abundant life God has created for us, so being connected is imperative. It opens us up to receive a new and more fulfilling current, or shall I say flow, in life.

Unlike other donor hearts, Jesus' heart is perfect. It also has the power to heal every other section of your life. Let's prepare our minds and hearts for the first surgery.

Heart Check

Here are a few questions for you to spend some time reflecting on. Allow yourself the peace of being completely honest with yourself, and with God. Do not judge yourself. Journal your responses.

- ♥ What are my core beliefs regarding Jesus' heart being sufficient to handle my imperfections and shortfalls? Why?
- ♥ What are some irrational beliefs I believe about myself, love, and my purpose?
- ♥ What makes you worthy? How do you determine if you are a success or failure?
- ♥ How do your beliefs about yourself compare and contrast to what Christ says about you? (Reference scriptures such Psalm 139 or Jeremiah 29:11)
- ♥ What are some truths about Christ that I need to embrace to prepare for this Divine Heart Transplant transformation taking place in my life?

♥ What are some things I must disconnect from to make room for the necessary connections I need to make for my life to change?

♥ Who are some people I must disconnect from to make room for the necessary connections I need for my life to change?

CHAPTER *10*

CHRONIC AILMENT OR ACUTE ISSUE?

Many of the issues that damaged my heart came about from socially and culturally accepted norms, that were, and still are, very damaging to our society. For this reason, many people often lack empathy when dealing with matters of the heart because they have been desensitized to these problems. They've become familiar with acute issues.

Step Two - Awareness

It's like growing up without a father. When I was a little girl I thought having a father living in the house with you was the best thing a child could possibly have. From elementary through middle school, I'll say about 80% of my friends and associates were raised in single parent homes with little or no contact with their fathers. No one talked about it in our group three-way phone calls (you remember those?). No one mentioned it when we met up. It was as if the way of living, without a father, was a normally acceptable occurrence. It wasn't until I was twenty-nine years old that I realized a chilling truth - this wasn't normal, or at least not the way God intended it to be when He first created the world. Broken homes were a result of the brokenness and sin of man. It touched my heart because it made me sad. It explained why many of our lives looked the way they did and why we were experiencing the pain we were experiencing. We expected it. We were accustomed to it. Our hearts were broken and we didn't even know.

This observation is not to condemn my upbringing or speak against the way I was raised. My mother did the best she could with what she had, and I love and appreciate her for it; however, looking back over my life, I can see the detriment that was inflicted on my generation--mentally, emotionally, and spiritually--by not growing up with a father's love and strength. Many of us had bad attitudes and got into unnecessary mischief, all as a silent cry for aggressive help. The cries fell on deaf ears. We needed a remedy for the pain. We still need to remedy the pain.

But who is capable of delivering a healing dose when it seems that most of us are not aware of the pain, or the cause of the pain that is acknowledged? An epidemic of fatherlessness being accepted as a social normalcy is an example of mass heart disease affecting millions, going undetected and untreated. Why would a physician diagnose a problem they deem normal or socially accepted? The truth is, this is only accepted by people who cannot relate to what having an absent parent feels like.

Heart failure usually manifests in two forms - problems with the heart pump function (most common) or a lack of electrical transmission throughout the heart (causing irregular beating). The same is true with your divine heart. Albeit personally or professionally, these are the main areas of failure for women: the ability to allow love to flow through life and the ability to allow that flow to continue constantly. When someone has a broken heart they often go into protection mode, becoming very hard to protect themselves, and essentially stop pumping. The other response is often shutting down and allowing people to run over them.

Let's break this down some. It's hard to continually open up and allow your love to flow when you're constantly being hurt. I experienced this form of heartbreak. I grew up very guarded with my true feelings and emotions because I did not feel safe enough to truly express myself. This is true with everyone-- except my grandmother. She was someone I felt like I could trust. I knew that she was an ally of my mother, but like

Switzerland, she was my ally, as well. I guess you can say she was a healing treatment for the both of us.

I have always wondered why we don't pay attention to our children, more specifically, how we treat and talk to them. As a parent, I've seen the damaging effects that demeaning and critical language has on children. I also know this to be true from a personal perspective.

For some strange reason, many of us seem to think the heartbreak we've experienced came from our first crush, or some other firsthand experience with love. That is almost never the case. There are countless studies that highlight how babies experience the emotions of their mothers. Even in the womb, joy, peace, frustration, and pain are all felt by babies before they even set eyes on the light of day.

Heart Check

I want you to take a pause and think about how this may have personally affected you. Honestly answer and journal your responses.

- ♥ Do you know what your mom was doing while she was pregnant with you?
- ♥ What was your family dynamic like as an infant?
- ♥ What type of environment were you raised in?
- ♥ Were you indirectly taught women are supposed to be strong and fearless without ever shedding a tear, or, were you taught that a woman is only supposed to have babies and serve her man? If neither, what were you taught a woman should be like?

Chapter 11

THE DANGERS OF LETTING GO

As you can see, this transplant process is no joke. Becoming aware of your ailments and the causes that created them is always a humbling experience. Are you feeling the pain and discomfort of the process now? As I researched the intricacies of the physical heart transplant, I found out this part of the transplant is the most dangerous-removing your old heart. The truth of the matter is this heart is already very weak and or badly damaged.

There is always scar tissue left behind from previous interventions done in failed attempts to save the heart. Scar tissue never returns to natural viable tissue. It actually weakens the heart and prevents it from operating at full capacity. I stress this point because I need you to understand what you are up against. You're too far in this process to look back now. As God, the Master Surgeon, removes your old heart of stone, there will be areas where you are weak that you've convinced yourself that you are strong in. These may cause complications. This is what scar tissue looks like.

You chose this particular surgeon because He is the master. He specializes in healing and restoring the worst cases of heart failure. Don't fear His imperfections by way of "spiritual malpractice." Instead, invest your energy and resources in the tools required for you to release your damaged dysfunctional heart. The Master can't make a mistake; therefore, malpractice is not even something He considers.

I know you may think this part of the process will be easiest, right? NO. It won't. The difficulty with releasing the old heart is releasing your current identity attached to it. You have a certain view of yourself. You, and others, have placed unfair pressures and expectations on your life due to some of the situations you've experienced. They need to be addressed and bypassed to make room for better expectations. Be honest with yourself. It hurts to see your own mess in the mirror. The DHT process not only exposes your mess, it forces you to let go of it, even if your dysfunction is all you've known.

As I coach clients through this process, it always blows my mind on how willing women are to admit their flaws; however, they are not as welcoming to solutions to remedy the problem. For example, I spoke with a very amazing woman one day. We were discussing relationships, and I shared my perspective on submission in marriage. She bragged about her strength and her ability to stand up to anyone, especially her husband. It was if she wore her independence and strong personality as a badge of honor.

I could relate to her. Though I could relate, it doesn't mean I now agree. Let me explain.

I used to define worth by my works. I started taking care of myself at age fourteen. I always wanted to be a kid, but I was my mom's only child, and I was always very mature for my age. I grew up strong. That strength was only a hard outer shell covering my brittle insides--emotions and self-image. Having to be so responsible hurt because it meant I wasn't being properly cared for by the ones who were responsible for me. I already told you how I felt about my father, but I hated my mother too. I loved her but it hurt. I wanted to stop loving her but I couldn't. She was my mom. She was my mom, but the men in her life seemed to always come before me. If you had asked me about this when I was younger, I would've told you that I was fine. The truth is, I truly questioned all of my value due to the fact that no one felt obligated to adequately care for and provide for me.

Now some will say, "What doesn't kill you makes you stronger," and I don't disagree with this statement. I will say that pain and trauma are real, and they result in the formation of scar tissue. I became tougher and toughness turned into resilience, but my heart was malfunctioning on the inside, for a very long time, and no one seemed to know. I struggled with seeing my beauty, and I couldn't appraise my worth. I was looking for others to do the appraising for me. I knew God's Word told me how much He loves me, but I honestly had difficulty seeing it for myself.

This constant bout with dysfunction and insecurity was wearisome. This type of buildup is what causes a heart to fail. This scenario is my own experience, but you may have experienced something similar. You have to mature to a place that allows you to heal. In order to heal you must accept the fact that you are sick and hurting. You are not invincible, and you want to be loved. This is not a sign of weakness; instead, this is proof that you are human, and most of all willing to do the work of God-love thy neighbor as you love thyself.

The defeated mindset that creates the buildup must be released during this procedure. You must let go of all of your old thoughts, ideas, rituals and habits that are a gateway to the life of broken heartedness you are leaving behind. These things damaged your heart before so you must let them go. You don't want old defects to infect your new heart.

The problem with letting these rituals of thoughts and actions go is that they have become a false sense of identity for you. You are not what you do, or have done. You are also not what you've been through. Many of us associate who we are with what we do. When you do things differently, or out of your normal routine, the defeated mindset/thought process will take you back to the environment or situation that is most familiar. This familiarity doesn't have to be desired or revered; it's just what is normal to you. Let me explain. You may be in an abusive relationship, but you continue to return to your abuser. You know the relationship is toxic, but you have stayed this long because you love him and he loves you, right? You love him even if it comes at the expense of your dignity, self-respect and possibly your life, right?

Step Three - Acceptance

The divine heart transplant forces you to confront and overcome the skeletons in your closet-the cause of your divine heart disease. This confrontation exposes where the skeletons came from and why they still remain, wreaking havoc in your life. Accepting your life for what it currently is and accepting yourself for who you are is critical in your journey to living and loving again. If you can't accept your part in your mess, you'll never truly heal and live the beautifully authentic life God created, formed and molded you to live. When seen from the proper perspective, acceptance is beautiful, if you allow it to be.

To accept, as defined by Google, is to believe or come to recognize (an opinion or explanation, etc.) as valid or correct. When you release your broken heart, you are accepting everything that happened to you as completely done. There is no more holding grudges or making people pay for what they've done to you. You must relinquish any desire to prove "them" wrong or compete with those you secretly feel inferior to.

To let go of a damaged heart means releasing fears and prejudices towards others, as well as yourself. Manipulation and jealousy must be denounced as you obtain your new heart, while many wrestle with even admitting they struggle with these heart issues at all. This is a major reason why so many women are living below their God-given potential. This is also why many have broken hearts operating at limited capacity.

I used to be this woman. I justified my wrongdoings and holding on to my pain. I didn't truly trust anyone, at the core, because I had such a history of being disappointed. My defeated mindset was that I needed to keep my expectations low because that's all I would experience. This mindset kept me in a cycle of hurt, pain and dysfunction, and I suspect it is doing the same to you.

When I visited the Master Surgeon, He advised me I would have to let go of my distrust, cynicism, skepticism and lack of faith. Yes. I was in church regularly, reading my Bible daily and fellowshipping with the saints, but the scar tissue had weakened my heart so much, I need greater intervention than the routine care I was receiving on Sunday mornings and Wednesday nights. My heart trouble took me to place where I could no longer get by on a quick fix of Jesus. It was like placing a bandage on a surgical wound. I would go to church and have emotional experiences, but go home and raise pure hell with my husband and children. I was envious and jealous. It wasn't who I was, but it was who I had become because I chose not to deal with the insecurities that snagged my identity. My new heart would remedy the jealousy and envy, but I had to accept who I had become in order to release her and embrace the new me by way of Jesus Christ.

I accepted Jesus ten years before I truly accepted the identity that comes with His salvation. He saved my soul, instantly, but it took me years to renew my heart by transforming my mind. As I work with women and support them as God transforms them through their transplant process, acceptance is the hardest part. Many of us have trouble admitting to and exposing our flaws and shortfalls. We've been taught vulnerability is a weakness, and hence choose to never be weak - at least not in the sight of others. In taking on this hard persona we never give our hearts an opportunity to excrete the toxins brought in through pain and brokenness. This is why so many women die from natural heart disease. They never exercise their hearts and find themselves sick and dying from a preventable illness. Yes. You may need to eat better and exercise more, however that won't get to the true source of your problem.

The truth is, you've probably been emotionally and mentally hurting. You probably don't even realize how much you've made yourself sick. It's imperative you release your broken heart. You can no longer hold on to your brokenness. You have to accept your weaknesses and their atonement through the sovereignty of God. This can only be done by you. The surgeon is a master, but you must furnish the will to live. He shall sustain you through this process. He will not let you drown, burn, or flat line. You will get weak through this surgery and the recovery process. Sometimes your weakness will feel like death pouncing on you. Do not fear. The Master Surgeon has never lost a patient. He is perfect, His perfection allows you to accept yourself and all of your idiosyncrasies, as well as your own perfections.

Heart Check

Take some private quiet time to reflect on these questions. Honestly answer; journal your responses.

- ♥ What areas of your life have you been reluctant to confront? Why?
- ♥ What negative habits and thoughts are you repeating that are causing dysfunction in your life? (This includes but is not limited to dietary, attitude, and financial habits)
- ♥ Have you been more committed to maintaining who you used to be than you've been to nurturing who you are becoming?

Chapter 12

COMPASSION VERSUS TOLERANCE

You were created to thrive in this lifetime. Romans 8:18 reminds us that our lives were not intended solely for suffering. We are supposed to glory and enjoy life as well. One of the toughest parts of me accepting my mess and the part I played in my dysfunction was the difficulty I had giving and receiving compassion. I tolerated people because I had to. This was one of the symptoms of my heart disease. The hardening of my heart caused me to limit my interactions with people I deemed difficult. I thought it was the correct thing to do in order for me to truly heal. I knew that life gives back whatever you give off, but I did not realize the power motives release into our lives - the Spirit of God knows and the Word of God discerns the thoughts and intentions of our hearts (Hebrews 4:12 ESV).

As I journeyed through my transplant process, I struggled with being able to accept my downfalls. I had justifications for my mistakes, but I wanted others to be accountable for their actions. My mom and I had a tense relationship for over 15 years. I justified my lack of patience with her because she never seemed to have patience with me. I tolerated her because she was my mom, but I really did not want anything to do with her. I hated spending time with her, and I was not very nice when we were in one another's presence. I had deep-seated anger for her that I was denying. I had verbally forgiven her with my mouth, but I was in denial about the hurt, pain and disappointment she caused, so I was not ready to forgive in my heart, and definitely not willing to forget.

To forget, during the forgiveness process, is not a realistic aspiration seeing as we never truly forget anything. This is what makes forgiveness so critical. Because we will always remember the incident, no matter what, we must be careful to remind ourselves of our choice to forgive, especially when the residue of the pain is still present. If I'm honest, I wanted to make my mother pay for the pain I endured while I was a child under her care. I knew it was wrong to feel that way, but I couldn't help myself. I secretly wanted her to suffer, the way I did. Nothing I ever did was good enough for her, so why should I give grace to her if she's never given it to me?

I was tolerating her. I had no compassion. I had no compassion for her because I did not have any for myself. I was irritated with myself, so others always got on my nerves. This thought process seemed acceptable until I had an epiphany one day. I heard the Lord whisper in my inner ear, "How can you expect others to express patience and compassion towards you when you won't return the favor? Others need grace the same way you do." It was as if the Lord Himself sat me down to make me understand a truth that had been previously eluding me. I must accept my mess before focusing on the messiness of others. I must not tolerate my mother, withholding compassion, if I want others to have compassion for me. This way of being requires authenticity and vulnerability.

Often we hold back love, commitment, and creativity in hopes to receive an investment prior to making one. Life doesn't work that way. Our compassion, as well as love, cannot be offered conditionally. Jesus freely died on a cross for our sins. He did not wait until we were good enough, or until we cleaned up enough to be acceptable. No. He loved us right where we were and died for our sins, even the secret ones that nobody else knows about. He did not tolerate you. He loved you so much He was able to show compassion through His death on the cross. Consider this compassion as you journey through the process. Your heart donor, Jesus, gave His life so you can have a new heart that allows you to thrive here on earth. As you receive life-giving compassion, be sure to gauge yourself to ensure that you are not just tolerating others. Whatever you do, do it from a joyful heart.

The Never Ending Transplant

One of the things you have to be aware of is the constant emotional work required to live and love on a level you've never experienced. We've talked about the first three (3) steps of the divine heart transplant process--connection, awareness, and acceptance. You should now be clear on the necessary connections you need to make in order for you to begin to let go of your brokenness. First, you must embrace your wholeness in Christ and the purpose you were created to fulfill. This connection brings about a sense of awareness, in your inner being, that opens your eyes to see the traps, pitfalls, and misfortunes - the divine heart issues - that have been fueling these areas of dysfunction.

Upon becoming aware, your blind eyes begin to open up to the truth about your life and the world around you. You have to be willing to own your messes and evaluate your struggles, as well as the messages they create. Accepting who you are without any disclaimers makes room for more of your authenticity to be exposed. Your natural essence is beautiful-not the artificial dysfunction you've grown accustomed to existing in. Long gone are the days of you reinforcing others only to tear yourself down. The DHT process forces you to accept yourself for who you are, and in doing so, consequently, to begin to accept others the same way.

In order to truly heal and transform, you must be willing to extend to others the grace and mercy God has freely and consistently given to you. The book of James talks about ways to authentically express your faith. You, like myself, may have been hurt, violated, abandoned, and abused, but it doesn't justify you having a lack of compassion. Honestly, much of your broken heart disease has come from your inability to express compassion for yourself and others.

Grudges take up unnecessary space in your heart and mind. This space turns to scar tissue that eventually becomes useless.

Wherever scar tissue is, that scar tissue weakens your heart and prevents that particular part of your heart from being able to function. If you're a child of God, a follower of Christ, you are promised to be loved by Jesus, protected, and forgiven for all of your sins. The question is: do you have faith in this promise, and if so, why are you struggling with believing that He can do this for you? He's already done it for you; it is finished.

The Blame Game

One of the biggest obstacles to obtaining a new heart is letting go of all of the excuses, reasons, and explanations for the failures you've encountered. Your heart is broken. Stop trying to justify the brokenness that has dominated your life. Now is the time to remedy this nasty issue. Acceptance of your brokenness and disease is the foundation of healing.

I talked about many of the contributing factors to the divine heart disease that disturbed my life. My parents, my ex, my husband and my children were often the scapegoats I blamed for my frustration and unhappiness. In order for me to heal and overcome, I had to learn how to stop blaming those who hurt me and own my part in my pain. They were not the sole reasons for my life's downfalls.

Acceptance of who you are brings about an air of accountability. I used to blame my dad, and his absence, for my depression. I blamed my mom for my bad attitude. I blamed my husband for my loneliness, and I blamed my children for my stress and financial strain. I blamed others for not being there for me, without realizing that I wasn't being there for myself. How could I possibly expect others to invest in, support and love me when I refused to do these things for myself?

Blaming others for the pain you've experienced is like being angry at the waiter in a restaurant if you decide to overeat. All he did was serve you what you ordered, or in most cases, thought about. It was your decision to eat your fill, or not. Most of the pain and dysfunction we exist in is a product of an unwillingness to own our personal defects and shortfalls. I am not saying that you are wrong or that you're to blame for what happened in your life. I am saying that you have to accept whatever took place because you cannot change the past. You also have to consider the idea that your perspective of the situation in question may have been distorted due to your point of view. This distortion brings about an inaccurate representation of the possibilities and potential of your healing, as well.

Let me give you an example. I used to blame my mom for my low self-esteem and for my father being absent. I convinced myself it was her fault because I lacked self-confidence and self-love. I never took the time to challenge my own limited belief system, my mindset, and discover why I had such a deficit of self-worth. It wasn't until I started the DHT process that I realized I was blaming my mother for my own personal feelings towards myself. In reality, I was solely to blame for what I was thinking-not others-because of what I assumed they were thinking and saying about me. I didn't have a healthy self-image, and it was up to me to remedy this sickness, by the grace of God. I never wanted to take ownership of my pain because I didn't want to accept the part I played in my own pain.

It's easy to blame and convict others for trespasses, but it's honorable and right to shine that light of judgment right back on yourself. Matthew chapter seven talks about focusing on your own flaws before you point out the shortcomings of others. This allows you to truly get to know yourself and what makes you tick. If you're always blaming others, you will never be able to see yourself, and seeing you is vital to the healing and transformation process. You can only change yourself - you empowered by Christ.

I know life would be easier if everyone thought and did things like you, but that isn't healthy, nor would it be realistic. Being accountable for everything about you-flaws, failures, and triumphs-allows the Master Surgeon to properly disconnect your identity and vitality from the heart that's been damaged by your past, and current, trauma and pain.

If you're blaming others for your sickness, you'll also have to credit them for your healing. No one, but God, has that type of power over you unless you willingly give it to them. You have the power!

Heart Check

Take time to reflect on the questions below. Be brutally honest with yourself as you think about your answers. Journal your responses.

- ♥ What area(s) of your life are hurting and/or struggling the most? (Mentally, physically, relationally, financially, etc.)
- ♥ Are you blaming others for the pain you are currently experiencing?
- ♥ If you are honest, what person/people do you blame for most of the heartache you've been experiencing? Why do you blame them?
- ♥ What area(s) of your life do you need to accept and be accountable for the role (s) you've played in your pain?
- ♥ What difficulty are you having with accountable for your actions, or the lack thereof?
- ♥ What untruth have you believed about yourself that you need to release in order to embrace the truth about your life and God's will for you? (For example, "I'm not good enough." or "I'm not worthy.")

CHAPTER *13*

DISCONNECTING FROM THE DISEASE

How are you doing? Just like with any other procedure, I want to check on you and make sure you are still responsive through this transformation you're undergoing. We're halfway through the transplant. If you're struggling with accepting who you are and what you've done, it's okay. This type of guilt and shame is to be expected. Confrontation often starts off difficult and gets better with time. All I'm saying is, don't give up now.

Transplants are not available to every patient who possesses a failing heart. One of the reasons you embarked upon this journey is because the Master Surgeon spiritually and emotionally "cleared" you for this procedure. Just like medical clearance needed by a physician, spiritual clearance assured you were prepared for this process. Everyone can't handle the type of vulnerability, authenticity, and surrender it takes to undergo a DHT, and sadly, this why so many women choose to live in pain and dysfunction. They would rather suffer in silence than live in the comforts of peace.

You can't stop at this point. You don't have to question your ability to make it through the entire procedure because you received your clearance. Stopping here means death. Aborting this mission means the death of purpose and vision on the other side of your pain.

You've accepted that your life's problems and dilemmas weren't totally everyone else's fault. I know that was tough. I encourage you to journal your emotions and fears as you journey through. I also do not want you to feel as if I'm encouraging you to condemn yourself (as if you haven't already done that enough). The truth hurts. It hurts even more when you find out the truth about yourself. Finding out the truth about yourself is the pinnacle of your transplant process. It's also the most impactful. This is the point where God detaches you from who you thought you were. Now is the time to FORGIVE.

Your Master Surgeon is equipped with the ability to detach you from the defeated mindset and lifestyle you've existed in. No longer will you hold on to the idea that you're not good enough. Gone are all the days of living below your means and secretly doubting your capabilities. When you forgive yourself, and others, you can embrace the identity God created you to embody.

STEP FOUR - FORGIVENESS

You may currently consider yourself someone who is strong and independent, but if you'd be honest, this wall of strength has guarded a brittle and wounded heart. The disappointments you've experienced hurt you to the core. Did you ever admit to anyone how bad it hurt? I know I did not for a very long time. I did, however, convince myself to become more independent and evasive with my emotions. Reason being, I never truly trusted anyone with my heart. I learned this defense mechanism as a little child.

I've heard it said "living in unforgiveness is like you drinking a poison and expecting someone else to die from it." Unforgiveness is one of the main contributors to divine heart failure. I prided myself in holding grudges and getting revenge. I thought I was being responsible for myself by taking matters into my own hands. Paul tells us, in the book of Romans, that vengeance is for the Lord, not us. This stage in the process was very sobering for me. I came face to face with my dysfunction, and it didn't feel good.

I had many issues with many people that needed to be resolved. Since I had accepted Christ 10 years earlier, I had convinced myself I had forgiven these people. Intellectually I said I forgave my mom and dad, but my heart was diseased with unforgiveness. I had convinced myself that I was fine. I honestly believed I had made amends with my parents, my ex and others who had wronged me. It wasn't until the surgeon opened me up and started removing my damaged heart that I realized how bad the disease of unforgiveness had limited my ability to love and be loved.

Can you relate to this? Have you been trying to convince yourself you've forgiven someone, maybe your spouse or one of your parents, but you know there is still enmity within your heart? Don't deny or avoid this issue. Addressing this issue is the difference between life and death in your relationships, career and even your health. You can pray, fast, speak in tongues and speak prophecy over others, but if you don't forgive others, as well as yourself, your work will be in vain.

Ouch! That hurts but it's a healing antidote to your years of brokenness, dysfunction and pain.

Let me be clear, I was surrounded by people who loved me, but I often felt unloved. This feeling of gloom was a direct product of unforgiveness. I didn't forgive others easily because I was neglecting to forgive myself. I blamed myself for most of the misfortune I experienced. This self-crucifixion started at a very young age, around four or five years old. I was convinced it was my fault my dad was not around I thought I must've done something wrong to make him stay away. I also felt inadequate because my mom often seemed to be unsatisfied, and for whatever reason, I blamed myself for her unhappiness. I came to the conclusion that I wasn't good enough and I was bad to the core. I was pretty, smart, athletic, and usually kind to others, but I did not see my worth. Low self-esteem caused me to limit my potential, and I was angry with myself for feeling this way.

I knew better. I knew what the word said. "I am fearfully and wonderfully made" is what Psalms 139 tells us, but I couldn't digest the pill of truth because of the hardness of my heart. The lack of forgiveness of myself, and others, was causing me to reject my own healing. This created barriers that slowed me down as I prepared my heart to be strong enough to withstand the DHT process. I was so feeble in the arena of forgiveness it almost killed me. The scary thing was I didn't have a clue of how sick I was. Unforgiveness is a silent killer that robs its victims of a fulfilling life with joy to the fullest. It is truly a thief that steals. Thankfully Jesus is the redeemer. This is why the transplant process is imperative. Receiving Jesus' heart allows your heart to heal and be well. This can't take place until you release your old broken heart. That heart cannot be released until you completely commit to forgiveness.

Forgiveness doesn't mean you won't still hurt at the thought of the situations that have hurt you, and those who've wronged you. It does mean you are detaching yourself from continuing to hurt and stay sick from this chronic condition. A chronic condition is a disease that you live with, but it isn't aggressively being treated. A disease that is chronic would be hypertension, or also known as high blood pressure. This can prove to be deadly over a long period of time, but isn't aggressively treated initially. It's managed over time, though never going away. An acute disease is one that needs attention immediately. A chronic issue, over time, can become acute. Years of holding on to pain caused your heart to fail. The chronic illness caused an acute disease. Forgiveness allows you to release disease and make room for your new thriving heart in Christ.

The Peace in Letting Go

Philippians 4: 6-7 says, "Do not be anxious about anything, but in everything by prayer and supplication with thanksgiving let your requests be made known to God. And the peace of God, which surpasses all understanding, will guard your hearts and your minds in Christ Jesus." You must be willing to tell yourself a new story so that you are able to let go of the old, debilitating one.

You are now letting go of your prejudices. You must, in order to move forward with your transplant. God will give you a peace to be able to forgive, accept, become aware, and connect to Christ and a better life than what you're accustomed to. As a strong woman, forgiveness could be difficult for you because you may equate it with reconciliation. I'd beg to differ.

When God gives you the peace to forgive, He doesn't command you to reconcile. If you know someone is toxic for you, you may want to refrain from pursuing reconciliation.

I understand if you've decided not to pursue reconciliation is due to someone being abusive, however I want you to be sure you are truly not harboring unforgiveness, and consequently an unwillingness to overcome your past hurt.

What I will tell you is: do not quench your spirit. If you desire to reconcile after you have forgiven, or have been forgiven, don't make your desire about the other person; instead, make it about you and Christ. This assures that your efforts aren't superficial or conditional. Love on others even if they do not express the same love to you in return. Remember, Jesus told us whatever we do for the least of men we are doing unto him.

The transplant process teaches you how to be more sensitive to your environment and the world around you. Peace allows you the connectedness of spirit, mind and body, to best operate in life while overcoming your broken heart. It's worth it for you to overcome, at all costs.

Do not hold back in your pursuit of peace. It makes forgiveness that much better. Peace allows you to release all connections to the old you, along with the brokenness and dysfunction that once came packaged with you. Forgive yourself. Forgive those who've hurt you. Forgive everyone else and make room for your new heart and the way of living that accompanies it.

It's Scary

This is a very difficult time in the transplant process. You will experience emotions from excitement to shame. It is imperative that you do not avoid the difficult areas in your past that you tried to cover up. These key areas must be addressed so you don't contaminate your new heart with a diseased mentality. You may have to make phone calls and house calls to those you once thought you would never speak to again.

I know it can be intimidating, or downright scary, to think about confronting those who've hurt you, and the ones you've hurt. I want you to ease your mind. Allow God to lead you in the right direction. You will know when you need to move forward and how you need to proceed. Your Master Surgeon has a first assistant, the Holy Spirit, who makes sure you know the right information to live triumphantly through the transplant process, and post operatively. It's up to you to act on this knowledge.

You will also feel joy and pride as you begin to shed away the damage that has broken your heart. When I began to forgive those who'd hurt me - friends, family, exes - I realized I was stronger than I had given myself credit. I felt a liberty in my heart that empowered me to make other powerful changes in my life.

Don't let your old mindset convince you to skip this part of your process. You absolutely need to release your past baggage to make room for your future blessings. Ask yourself if holding grudges from your past is worth you missing out on an abundant life in your near future?

Heart Check

Take time to reflect on the questions below. Be honest with yourself and journal your responses.

- ♥ What are your feelings about forgiveness?
- ♥ Who are some people you need to explore forgiveness concerning your relationship(s) with them?
- ♥ Are you holding unforgiveness towards yourself? If so, why?
- ♥ What areas of your life bring about the most shame for you?
- ♥ Is there anyone you need to ask for their forgiveness? If so, why haven't you asked them?

Chapter 14

THE DECISION TO LIVE

You have finally released your old hardened heart. Whew! In a natural heart transplant the patient is now connected to a heart-lung bypass machine as the surgeon prepares to attach the donor heart. This same procedure applies to the divine heart transplant process. As our Heavenly Father, the Master Surgeon, proceeds to connect you to your new heart, you will experience a period of bypass. The Lord will hold you up and assist you supernaturally to overcome your former deceptive identity in brokenness to embrace your new authentic identity in Christ.

This season of your life will be very awkward. You are not the person you once thought you were, yet you are definitely not where you desire to be. You're just passing by, in the bypass state. This is the time for you to take the initiative and make some decisions. You have gone through the sobering steps of connecting to the Master Surgeon, and becoming aware of who you are, or who you thought you were. This can cause pain and discomfort due to the rawness that develops around wounds as awareness becomes very abrasive.

In step three, you used the grace of God to begin to accept your issues revealed by the Holy Spirit. This is where you began to accept situations for what they are, and people for who they are. Self-acceptance causes you to let go of prejudices, grudges, and shame that have weighed you down for years. Acceptance is freeing because no one can blame or burden you with guilt once you are clear about where you stand in life.

Though all of these steps are imperative to follow, they do not feel good. Do not be surprised when your life begins to shift as a result of your voluntarily submission to God and the transplant process. You will cry when God shows you things about yourself you didn't know existed. It's okay. He is purging you to prepare you for the prosperity to come that is only found in and through Him.

Just like with any other surgery, you are under heavy anesthesia as you journey through this transplant. You must mentally prepare for the pain you will feel when the medication wears off. The Master Surgeon is holding and monitoring you right now. After you heal, you'll begin to develop pain management techniques that support your heart, instead of damaging it.

The fourth step we covered was forgiveness. This is the maturation step where you'll find yourself having to be the bigger person--a lot. You will find yourself needing assistance from the Surgeon to deal with life going on around you. You can do it. I know it's tough. If it was easy, everyone would be happy and fulfilled.

I wanted to recap the previous steps in order to prepare you for what's to come. Let's discuss Step five.

Step Five - Decisions to Change

One of the main reasons for a failing heart or ailing health is the unwillingness for many patients to change their lifestyle. This lifestyle that brought about the heart disease - swelling, aching, pain, and consequently, heart failure, has claimed the lives of millions, while terrorizing millions more. In order to avoid damaging your new donor heart and to prevent future heart failure, you must be prepared to make some serious, life-enhancing decisions. Making a decision is imperative to you receiving your donor heart and advancing through your life victoriously.

Let me give you an example of how detrimental not taking this step can be to a successful divine heart transplant. When I was in my first serious relationship, I constantly followed the steps of this transplant process, to a certain point. I would say that I was leaving him after every breach of trust that took place in our relationship, but I easily gave up after getting to step four, forgiveness. When I would find out about him cheating, it hurt so bad it would send me back to God. My heart would ache, literally drop to the floor, and I would run back to reestablish my connection with Him.

I don't know if you've ever experienced heart attacks caused by being hurt in a relationship, but it HURTS. I needed God every time. It wasn't until I realized my own power did this vicious cycle break. That reconnection would rejuvenate and recharge me so that I could begin to pursue relief.

I began to become aware of situations and circumstances all around me that my insecurities and brokenness often shielded me from being able to view. This enlightenment would lead me to a place of acceptance. I would begin to accept our toxic relationship for what it was and vow to move on to better opportunities for love. Let me be clear, I did not realize I was working these steps earlier in my life. As I reflected over my life, I began to notice the patterns. Truly making a decision was something I learned to do later in life.

I didn't like being angry with him nor did I like having turmoil with the random women he chose to cheat with, so I used the first three steps of this process to get to a place of forgiveness. I was trying to forgive him, and forget the women, in an effort to remedy my already brittle and volatile heart. This seemed like a good idea but it wasn't.

I didn't truly value myself, or even understand the magnitude of my worth. I was in a vicious cycle of being hurt by the same person who was nursing my wounds. It was hurtful. It was hurtful and heavy. It was consuming. I would say I was done, but after a few days, weeks, or months of "Baby, I love you" and "I'll never do it again" there comes a time when one must choose self-love and self-worth over self-sacrifice for the sake of insecurity.

I kept going back because I hadn't made a decision to be better and to demand more for my life. The lack of decision-making was the catalyst to the dysfunctional cycle I was in. I would not confront and deal with my problems, so they ultimately came and dealt with me. My brokenness led me to live in a state of self-sabotage for years. If you've ever stayed in a bad relationship for far too long, you know what I am talking about. This lifestyle choice weighs you down and tears away at your self-esteem. Making a decision broke that cycle of dysfunction for me, though that decision was as tough as nails.

I watched my mom, and other women I strongly admired, cycle through similar relationship patterns and dysfunctions. These accepted norms didn't feel good, but they were accepted, and consequently expected by me and so many women around me. When I realized I had the power to choose life and peace, not war and death, I took my life back and began to exit the dungeon of despair while, at the same time, releasing my damaged and diseased heart.

You may not have gone through tumultuous breakup cycles in your relationships, but you may struggle with trying to find your worth in material possessions or the works of your hands. Whether you're an overachiever, or a docile servant, you know God loves you and He is there with you. The problem is you've been having trouble embracing the possibility of your greatness, and you're having a difficult time breaking out of your not-so-comfortable comfort zone. Making a decision breaks your normal routine. It's you taking a stand and saying "ENOUGH IS ENOUGH" in your mind and commanding your heart to follow suit.

If you've been trying to prove yourself through the status you achieve or the money you're earning, you'll eventually burn yourself out. What you need is the heart and mind of Christ, your divine heart Donor, and everything else will fall into place. In order to receive the mind of Christ you have to accept Him into your heart and make a decision to do whatever it takes to allow His ways to saturate and permeate through your life. This requires commitment.

As the Master Surgeon begins the third and final surgery, connecting the donor heart to you, He's disconnecting you from the heart-lung bypass machine that's been temporarily keeping you alive. I had moments where God took complete control of me because I had nothing at all to give. Let this bypass machine represent all of the petty, simple, and unflattering habits you've developed over your lifetime, along with this process of transforming from brokenness to healing. Things like being easily offended, manipulative, and prideful must be surrendered during this part of the process. Disconnect from these habits so they won't contaminate your new heart and the lovely life you'll develop due to your DHT.

You have more control over your environment than you've given yourself credit for. When you decide definitively that you will overcome, break through, live without limits, stop being abused, elude poverty, transcend discrimination, etc., you become a force to be reckoned with. The heart of Christ can handle that demand of faith. Your old broken heart would fold under the pressure.

Decide to embrace the changes that your new heart will introduce to your life. Your friends and fantasies will begin to change. Things you desired to do before won't be as appealing as they used to be. You'll begin to feel sorry for the people you once envied. When people begin to "act funny" with you, don't take it personally. Accept the fact that they can feel your energy and that energy has been newly intensified. They know you mean business, and you don't have any more time for foolishness. Become okay with feeling awkward. You are shedding a false identity to embrace your authentic essence. You've come this far in the transplant process. There is absolutely NO looking back now.

"I think myself happy, King Agrippa, because I shall answer for myself this day before thee touching all the things… "Acts 26:2 KJV

Think Yourself Happy

As you embrace your new heart you must embrace the attitude and mindset that goes with it. Too often we sit around waiting for someone else to make us happy, not realizing that happiness comes from within. Though I experienced serious trauma in my life, as I'm sure you or someone you know has, the DHT process taught me the power of a positive, happy, joy-filled mindset. It's life-altering. Better yet, it's life-enhancing. This heart transplant truly changes things.

When I made the decision to adopt the heart of Christ, I realized how negatively focused my life was. I would encourage others, but I often expected the worse for myself. I was going to church every Sunday, living the Christian life (whatever that means), but continuing to doubt the power of God in my life. I doubted the power of God for myself because I honestly thought I wasn't good enough to truly be happy.

I knew what the Bible said about my predestined existence (Romans 8:29-30) and how my being was fashioned before time (Psalm 139). I had such low-self-esteem and self-worth that I struggled with the idea of God doing exceedingly and abundantly more than I could ask for (Ephesians 3:20). I believed He was capable. I just didn't believe it was for me. I had done too much. I hadn't completely forgiven myself. This defeated mindset caused me to stay in those vicious cycles of hurt and pain for most of my life. Whatever you think of yourself will manifest in your life. If you think you aren't worthy, life will affirm that mindset. If you believe that money is the root of all evil, you probably have strained financial relationships. Whatever you truly think about is what will show up in your atmosphere. This is why you must make a decision to think yourself happy and begin to find joy in every situation in your life, even in times of trial.

I know you're probably thinking, "How am I supposed to be happy with all of the mess and hurt that I'm experiencing in my life?", and I'm glad you asked. This step requires you to adopt new lifestyles and regimens that welcome joy and happiness. Create a space in your heart that allows you to thrive. Decide to embrace who you are becoming. Release who you thought you were.

In Christ we are all made new. Without Him we are dead to sin and the brokenness of this world. Jesus said, "I have told you these things so that in Me you may have peace. In this world you will have trouble. But take heart! I have overcome the world. (John 16:33 NIV)".

The real truth is we live in a fallen, broken and sinful world. We will always experience hurt and brokenness, until those of us in Christ transition to heaven. We do not have to identify ourselves with brokenness once we find our identity in Christ. That is why this transplant process is so vital. You need to have the heart of Christ so that you can adapt His identity as yours. Your trials here on earth are only momentary, your fulfillment in Christ are eternal. (2 Corinthians 4:17)

Start From the Top

One of the greatest decisions I've ever made was to develop a morning routine. How you start your day matters. As you receive your new heart, choose to be happy and peaceful by starting your day with Christ. He is your heart donor. Starting your day with Him assures that you'll have great heart health moving forward on your journey to living and loving again.

I want you to have practical tools to use as you make sound decisions to enhance your life. Here are six steps to help you get adjusted to your new heart and effectively start your day:

1. ***In All Things Give Thanks.*** Welcome every morning with thanksgiving. The Bible advises us to give thanks in all things (1 Thes. 5:18). Many of the perils we experience in life are brought about by way of pessimism. Jesus gave thanks to His heavenly Father before the two fish and five loaves of bread were multiplied to feed the 5000 (John 6:11-14). Giving thanks multiplies whatever you're thankful for, or complaining about, for that matter. Worrying is just a negative form of giving thanks. It's actually giving thanks for what you don't want. Think about that. When you give thanks for what you have, no matter how small or insignificant it may seem, God notices that He can trust you and bless you with more. Many people complain about not having enough money, time and

resources. When you learn to be grateful, especially for the little things, God will multiply those blessings. If all you focus on is negativity, negativity is what you will continue to receive.

2. **Be Still.** Take some time every morning to meditate and get quiet before God, if only for five minutes. This is time for your mind to stop wandering and take a break. I know that it's early in the morning, but that doesn't stop you from worrying about being on time to work, the condition of traffic, or what you will cook for dinner. All of those concerns have a place, however, your initial thoughts of the day shouldn't be contaminated with stressors. That is why it's so important to devote this quiet time to reconnect with Christ and listen to the Holy Spirit speak. Take deep rotating breaths inhaling through your nose. Hold your breath for 1-2 seconds (whatever works for you), and exhale through your mouth. Do this for 2-5 minutes starting out and work your way up to at least 15 minutes per day. Your mind will naturally wander as you breathe so focus on hearing yourself breathe to keep your mind on track. You can also listen to relaxing music, nature sounds, or guided Christian meditation to help keep your mind focused and relaxed. This time allows you to settle your soul and rejuvenate your heart. Settling your soul allows you to hear what God is speaking to you. Constant mental stimulation often drowns out the voice of God in our spiritual ears. Getting still allows you to tune your heart to the frequency of God. It heals and helps to prevent future sickness and disease. We are constantly praying to God, letting Him know what we want and how we feel. When you are still, you can hear His response to your prayers and so much more.

3. **Pray.** Prayer is a vehicle for us to communicate with God. Take time daily to communicate with the one who

love and cares for you. Philippians 4:6-9 tells you not to be anxious for anything, but in everything, through prayer and supplication with thanksgiving, make your request known unto God. God is great and all knowing, yet He still desires for us to be active participants in our relationship with Him. After you've given thanks, and spent some quiet time with God, now it's time to pray. It's imperative that you set the tone of your day with prayer. Since you've already set the atmosphere, your prayers will flow and be more sincere versus just being a list of requests made to some faraway genie of a creator. Prayer has different components that make it effective. Make sure you have reverence for God at all times. Begin your prayers with statements of God's sovereignty. Say something like this "Our Father in Heaven" or "Great and mighty God" to show your respect for Him. Next, offer worship. Thank God for who He is every time you speak with Him. He loves you unconditionally; begin to reciprocate that love in your communication with Him. Cry out to God and tell Him how you feel. Thank Him for His awesomeness and omnipotence. After you worship begin to make your petitions known to God. Tell Him what you want while believing in your own heart that He can and will provide. Be bold and specific while you pray. Do not lower your expectations for fear of disappointment. You are a child of the God of the universe. You were created to praise, worship and believe God for all of your provision. The bible says that we have not because we ask not (James 4:3). Take time to ask God for what you want and for what God has for you. Now that you've made your petition, give thanks. Thank God for hearing and answering your prayers, in advance. He loves you, and He's forcing you to love yourself through your private time with Him. Prayer changes things. Prayer changes YOU. It also maintains a healthy heart and prevents future wear and tear.

4. ***Read.*** Take time to read God's word every day. The word of God is living and breathing. His word is sharper than any two edged sword (Hebrews 4:12). As we commit to living a new transformed life with our transplanted Divine Heart we must take the proper medication to maintain health. The holy Word of God helps keep us on track and exposes us to ourselves. It also offers practical tools on how to live life to the fullest no matter the turmoil or opposition you may be facing. The Bible is the instruction manual to living life, literally and figuratively, and must be utilized daily for victorious, productive living.

5. ***Journal your life.*** Habakkuk 2 tells us to write the vision and make it plain. Life and death is in the power of that tongue, as well as the point of your pen or pencil. Journaling saved my life as I journeyed through the transplant process. When I was a little girl, I had a diary with a lock and key. I understood the purpose of a diary as a little girl, but I also know that it wasn't safe to write how I truly felt in my journal. At an early age, around 6-8 years old, I learned, through the responses of others, that telling the truth wasn't always accepted by adults. People ask for the truth but often are hurt and offended by hearing it. This fear of authentically expressing myself caused me to hold on to the pain, heartache, defeat, guilt, shame all because I didn't want to offend others. I literally almost killed myself because I didn't know how to properly release my stress. Journaling changed that for me. I started writing down my fears, hurts, dreams, visions and more. I uncovered details about myself that I would've never known existed if I hadn't been vulnerable enough to expose my innermost thoughts and feelings. I found my identity through the pages of my journal, and I also surrendered the mistaken identity I once embraced as my own.

Mentally dump through the pages of your journal. And if you're too afraid that someone will read your journal, burn it after you write it. Just get whatever is in you out, so that you can triumphantly continue your journey to living and loving again.

6. ***Get Moving.*** Everything you do, offer it to the Lord. One of the biggest reasons for heart failure amongst women is the lack of physical activity. We don't move enough to burn off the excess energy we possess in our bodies. When I incorporated a morning workout regimen in my daily routine my life truly jump started. I found myself having more energy and thinking more clearly throughout the day. Taking time to move my body at least five days a week actually made me start to care more about myself because I noticed the peace and relaxation my body felt as I released so much frustration and tension through exercise. Keep your mind and body renewed through getting active. Everything done for God is a form of praise, even if it involves you toning your physique.

I am not a health professional. Consult your health professional before you take time to implement these steps into your lifestyle. These are small steps you can take to begin to see big changes in your life. I encourage you to wake up 30 minutes earlier each day and take at least 5 minutes to complete each step. Overtime, you'll begin to experience transformation in your heart, mind, as well as your body. Many others will not take the time to implement these changes - that's why so many women are living broken, defeated, dysfunctional lives. They are doing the same things over and over but expecting different results. That type of behavior is defined as insanity. Adopting these new daily habits will help you prevent insanity and brokenness from consuming your life by training you to take on the mind of Christ.

Commitment

You've made the decision to undergo this transplant and it's now complete. The Master Surgeon has connected you to the heart of Christ. This is amazing, however that doesn't mean that everything will be perfect moving forward. This road to recovery requires a true commitment to transformation from you. Like we discussed earlier, you've been here before. You made promises to change and no longer tolerate the disappointment, hurt, and pain you once accepted as normal. But you've done this before.

This time will be different. You have to remain committed to your decision to end that toxic relationship no matter how good of a person he can be or how much he promised he loves you. You must stay committed to your promise when wanting to satisfy your insecurities and feelings of unworthiness. This is the part of the process where you feel the burn of transition, or walking these steps out.

Making a commitment cuts off all focus on distractions and/or options for retreat. You've embodied the heart of Christ, and now it's time to acclimate His heart into your life and lifestyle. Embracing His heart helps to transform your mind. Transformation of your mind ensures a healthy recovery and reduces your risk of postoperative rejection.

Heart Check

Take time to get to know yourself. Pay attention to your details. Journal the thoughts that immediately come to your mind as you ponder these questions.

- ♥ What areas of your life do you need to make a commitment to change? (Consider your thought life, finances, relationships, etc.)
- ♥ What decisions do you need to commit to in order to see success in your life moving forward?

♥ In what areas of your life have you been avoiding making definitive decisions?

♥ Why are you neglecting these areas?

♥ What are some commitments that you can make in your life that will create space that nurtures and allows you to transform into your God-given identity?

♥ Who or what do you have to disconnect from in order for you to create this space?

Chapter 15

THE RECOVERY PROCESS

I salute you for hanging in there through the entire Divine Heart Transplant process. I am so proud of you for not aborting the process before the end, limiting your own growth.

STEP SIX - TAKING ACTION

Though you now have a new healthy heart, you'll initially have more pain than you did when we started. This is a normal part of the recovery process. The same rules apply for cleaning up any mess. Whenever any major cleanup/restoration takes place, the mess always gets worse before it gets better. You were conditioned to life with a limited living capacity. Your life was adapted to accommodate dysfunction and this dysfunction brought about stiffness in your heart.

As you heal through this recovery process, expect to be exposed to truths about yourself, and the life around you that may cause you to want to give up. It's in these times you have to remind yourself of the work you've done to heal and the decision you made to exist in that healing until God calls you home.

This is the part of the process where your family, friends, and even your foes, will begin to remind you of who you used to be and everything you used to do. Do not allow their memories of your past to distract you from building your future. The road to recovery never ends so you must stay committed to taking continued action toward your complete recovery.

Use Caution

Previously I mentioned that there were two very dangerous steps in the transplant process. The first difficult step took place during the second surgery when we removed your damaged heart. The scar tissue and disease that led to heart failure also pose a threat when removing the damaged heart. The other difficult time is the recovery process.

Because the donor heart wasn't created inside of your body, your immune system is designed to destroy it, even though this new heart is keeping you alive. In natural heart transplants, most patients see failure in the postoperative portion of the transplant. The body will reject any organ that enters it if it didn't originate there. To prevent this type of rejection, transplant patients are forced to take certain anti-immunity medications for the rest of their lives.

These medications help prevent the body's immune system from rejecting the new heart they've received. Any recipient of a donor organ lives with this threat of rejection. They must all adopt new eating habits and lifestyle changes to support the success of their new heart.

The same rules apply for the DHT. Yes, you received the heart of Jesus, but it doesn't mean that you can kick your life into overdrive. You must become an active, willing participant in your life and the adjustments required to live victoriously.

Nothing truly matters until you take action. Up until this point, you've been doing a lot of observation and introspection. In this final step of the process, the surgery is over, but the road to recovery is just beginning. Your surgery is only as successful as your recovery process. The donor heart you've received is flawless -however, any return to your old way of existing - mentally, physically, and emotionally - can result in heart rejection and heart failure, again. It could also lead to death if not taken seriously. This part of the process is the least invasive part of the transplant, but could cause the most damage.

Take your healing seriously

Taking action exposes us to what we are truly made of. This part is hard because it forces you to be vulnerable. As you allow God to heal your heart, He leads, guides, and prepares you for life ahead. You will constantly find yourself facing tests and trials that once set you on edge. The Master Surgeon is making sure that your rehabilitation process is effective. It serves you no purpose to grow spiritually in the Lord but fail to use that knowledge and understanding in your everyday interactions with others. Taking action separates the haves from the have-nots and the miserable from the joyful.

Long after the surgery is completed you'll still have to keep your follow up appointments with the Surgeon. He has to make sure you're adjusting to your new heart. He makes adjustments to your post-operative treatment plan as needed. You may not always like the Doctor's orders, but you must comply if you want to live your life to full capacity.

You owe it to yourself to thrive in life. What good are you to God with a testimony of continued brokenness and defeat when you've been equipped for greatness in peace and health? Don't cause rejection of your new heart due to your unwillingness to detach from your defeated mindset. Detaching from this toxicity may cause you to find new friends and even relocate to a new city. You may find that you have to change the music you listen to and the books you read as you embrace your new heart. This process will expose you to the subconscious thoughts that have been consciously ruling your life, the ones that need to be adjusted.

As you take continued action, you will find the truth about yourself. This truth will allow you to love and respect yourself like never before. This journey isn't easy, though I wouldn't say it's hard, either. It definitely required a commitment to continued action, especially when you don't want to or feel like it. Remember that life is a like a marathon, not a sprint. You must stay in your lane and move through life at your own pace, while staying in God's will for your life.

Don't rush yourself to the finish line of healing. You will always have opportunities to heal because you will never know life without some form of pain. Your DHT allows you to properly process the pain by being able to find the joy and purpose in the midst of your sorrows.

Taking action allows you to get in and stay in the game of life versus being a sideline spectator. Spectators aren't usually exposed because they're on the sidelines but they also never get a chance to see their full potential because of the limited role they've chosen to play. Jesus sacrificed it all so you would be able to enjoy life to the full. Don't waste that investment on laziness. Laziness can cause damage to your new heart. An unwillingness to flow means blockage can reform and consequently cause your new heart to fail.

Don't allow former bad habits to hinder the promising future you have in Christ. Keep your heart healthy by keeping your blood flowing. Stay sensitive to the orders of the Surgeon. Your willingness to be actively compliant is directly related to your quality of life - joy, peace, love, and the pursuit of happiness.

Heart Check

You did not take this journey just to have bragging rights upon completion. Take some time to reflect on these questions and journal your responses.

- ♥ What have you learned about yourself during this transplant process that you did not know prior to reading this book?
- ♥ What immediate and consistent action do you need to take to continue to stay on your journey of living and loving again?
- ♥ Is this action new to you, or is this something you've been avoiding for a while?
- ♥ What are some of your fears regarding taking action in your life?

- ♥ What does a life of overcoming a broken heart and living and loving again look like for you?
- ♥ Are you willing to do whatever it takes for you to enjoy your life and live in divine purpose? Explain what you think the DHT will require of you.

CHAPTER *16*

LIFE AFTER A TRANSPLANT

I hope that you have found fulfillment and healing through the pages of this book. You no longer have to suffer through the limitations of divine heart disease, and ultimately, divine heart failure. God, the Master Surgeon, sent His Son, Jesus, to die for your sins, pain and heartache. My intention was to walk you through the divine heart transplant, expose you to the greatness inside of you, and help you overcome the pain that has generationally attacked your peace, potential, and prosperity.

I want to make sure you have the necessary tools to properly and successfully recover. Let's quickly recap the six steps of the divine heart transplant:

1. Connection - Don't try to be the lone ranger and suffer in silence. Establish the link between you and Christ. This connection is vital to you growing and overcoming the hurt that once had you down. Just like a cell phone, you must connect to your charger in order for your heart to have the power it needs to function properly. This is solely up to you. God is waiting for you to connect to him.

2. Awareness - Pay attention to the cycles and norms in your life. Are they healthy and productive for your current wellbeing and future success? Have you been living in a perspective that has limited your perception? Notice and acknowledge your triggers, habits, and behaviors. These are the symptoms of the divine heart disease you're confronting. Coming into

your awareness requires courage, authenticity and trust in Christ. You must begin to realize your issues before you can change them.

3. Acceptance - The first two steps serve as an anchor for the third. You must be anchored in order to successfully heal your life. Acceptance is a tough but necessary part of changing your life. Accepting the issues you have, and the part you've played in those issues, is one of the most important steps of this transplant process. Accepting the truth about you and your life from God's perspective prunes away excuses for continuing in emotionally, physically, and spiritually reckless behavior, and forces you to embrace all of who you are - good, bad and indifferent.

4. Forgiveness - Forgiveness is a critical step in the transplant process. It is imperative that you let go of any area of your life that is a snag preventing you from healing and moving forward. A heart can't heal if the one who possesses it refuses to forgive the offenders who hurt them. Many also struggle with forgiveness of themselves for the things they've done, and for what they did not do. Don't let that be you. You will be offended and hurt by others in this lifetime; it's inevitable. Focus on honing in on your connection to Christ as you embrace forgiveness. This fourth and crucial step is imperative for you to move forward in any situation in your life, especially dealing with matters of the heart.

5. Decision - Making a decision is the true catalyst in this process. Many times before you have gone through the previous four steps, but you often seemed to find yourself back in "that" situation, whatever it may have been. This is where you give

yourself a strategy. Look at the triggers, habits, and behaviors you once fell to. Choose to take another route when faced with adversity, disappointment, and offense. For example, if you are the type of person who allows people to treat you with disrespect because of your fear of not being loved, make a decision to stand up for yourself when you find yourself in a disrespectful situation. If you are prone to being quick to voice your opinion, you may have to decide to be quiet more often. You did not adopt your personality and behaviors in one day and it won't take just one day to overcome them. You have the strength to allow your heart to live and love, but you must first decide to unleash it.

6. Take Action - It's time to work out your new heart. You have taken all of the necessary steps to transform your life, now it's time to live the life you've desired all of your life. Taking action requires grit and resilience. You may want to give up, that will happen, but you must keep in mind that you have a strong heart ready to live on purpose. Set a strategy and allow God to lead you. Continued action keeps you healthy and allows you to gain momentum. Momentum is what you need to travel the journey of life. You have what it takes, just keep on taking it.

This transplant process demands authenticity and vulnerability. Now is not the time for you to be pretty, prim and proper. True deliverance can only come from a place of substance. One of the reasons we were so broken is because we were too focused on hiding and covering up our dysfunction. Many of us we taught, directly or indirectly, to "fake it until you make it" and we never learned how to just BE without any stipulations.

The Divine Heart Transplant process allows you to get to know and love yourself, especially the areas you once hid and despised. You may find yourself having to repeat these steps over and over throughout the recovery process. This is a sign that your heart is maintaining good health. The minute you stop working on yourself, you make yourself more susceptible to returning disease.

"Above all else, guard your heart, for everything you do flows from it."Proverbs 4:23 (NIV)

Your heart is wicked, yet it can only be judged by God. You were designed to be overflowing with joy, a joy that can only be given to you through Jesus, your Heart Donor. Ephesians 3:20 was promised to you; however, if you think you are not worthy to be happy, you'll never get to experience the exceedingly abundant life. That is the only downfall to the DHT. It renews your heart but not your mind.

Your mind must be renewed in order to live a life of victory and enjoyment in Christ (Romans 12:1-2). Work on your heart by committing to renewing your mind. Just as you renew your body daily through eating, exercise and good hygiene, dedicate a similar type of regimen to the renewal and development of your mind.

You need to be renewed from the inside out. Enough of looking pretty on the surface while secretly dying on the inside. Move forward with confidence knowing you have made the necessary sacrifices and commitments required, and therefore, paved a road for you to walk out your recovery on into your destiny.

Embrace every step of your process no matter what type of opposition may come. You have a Master Surgeon who has never lost a patient during a transplant. He surely won't fail in your case. Allow all support care services to help you along the way. Just as nurses, therapists and other physicians help out through the natural heart transplant process, God has placed people in your life to support you along your road to recovery. Do not allow pride to hinder your healing. Friends, therapists, coaches, family, spouses, children, siblings, hobbies, etc., are all support staff and services along your journey.

Don't despise your interactions with them; instead, appreciate how much they challenge you to be better, even if it doesn't feel good.

I'll be around to support you along your journey. We have a community of women who want to confront matters of the heart and live authentically on purpose, and I would love for you to join and do the same.

Let God heal your broken heart. It's your time to truly live and love again. And truth be told, you may be experiencing love for the very first time...

"For God so loved the world that he gave his only Son, that whoever believes in him should not perish but have eternal life." John 3:16

"For I will take you out of the nations; I will gather you from all the countries and bring you back into your own land. ²⁵ I will sprinkle clean water on you, and you will be clean; I will cleanse you from all your impurities and from all your idols. ²⁶ I will give you a new heart and put a new spirit in you; I will remove from you your heart of stone and give you a heart of flesh. ²⁷ And I will put my Spirit in you and move you to follow my decrees and be careful to keep my laws. ²⁸ Then you will live in the land I gave your ancestors; you will be my people, and I will be your God. ²⁹ I will save you from all your uncleanness. I will call for the grain and make it plentiful and will not bring famine upon you. ³⁰ I will increase the fruit of the trees and the crops of the field, so that you will no longer suffer disgrace among the nations because of famine." Ezekiel 36: 24 -30 (NIV)

ABOUT THE AUTHOR

Adelai Brown is a Heart Coach ™, radio show host, and community facilitator, focused on emotional wellness and personal growth. She uses her skills to teach, encourage and inspire others to confront matters of the heart and live authentically on purpose. After overcoming depression, teenage pregnancy, and domestic violence, she has devoted her life to helping others heal their inner wounds, and begin to live effective lives by cultivating their inherent greatness.

With the motto "Heal your heart - transform your life", Adelai has committed herself to teaching and mentoring women, men, and youth to confidently address the hidden issues of the heart, and use vulnerability as a strength to experience complete wholeness.

"We have to understand that being whole and living on purpose is the ultimate goal. If you don't know who you are, you will never live the life you were created to live. I'm in the business of exposing people to who they are, and the greatness that they possess within. We have to forget about who we thought we were and focus on exploring who we were created to be. We are not our past, but we must confront it in order to be able to move forward victoriously. We can truly do ALL things through Christ who strengthens us." she says.

Adelai is the founder of Heart Connections, a Christian personal development company based in Charleston, South Carolina. Coming from a background in healthcare, the healing and renewal of the hearts and souls of individuals and communities is the driving force of her movement. Her mission is to create lasting solutions that help individuals, families and communities overcome internal and external conflict. The five pillars of her company are: healing, enlightenment, authenticity, revitalization, and transformation. She strives to create effective content highlighting these pillars.

Adelai has self published three books, including her new book, *Help! Save Me from My Broken Heart Your Journey to Living and Loving Again,* a life-enhancing tool for individuals who want to totally transform their lives, which is available on her website, www.theheartconnections.com, and Amazon.com. She has created, written, and hosted multiple youth and adult workshops, retreats and summits.

In September of 2014, Adelai launched Heart Talk, a transformational empowerment session, that airs every Monday evening. Live on the air, she does coaching and discusses topics that range from *discovering your worth* and *how to overcome your past,* to *learning to be intimate through vulnerability* and *ways to overcome trauma and live triumphantly.*

She has delivered countless transformational speeches to audiences with a wide range of ages and demographic ages, and has contributed to various publications. Adelai is a co-founder of The Be Blessed! Daily Mentoring, a program based in Charleston, SC that mentors young people in 5th-12th grade. The mission is to inspire youth to employ their voices for positive change while living morally responsible lives, and possessing healthy self-images.

Adelai lives in Charleston, South Carolina with Her husband, Kevin. They have four children and two cats.

Connect with Adelai online at www.theheartconnections.com and on YouTube at http://bit.ly/heartconnections. To book her to speak to your audience and empower them to live authentically on purpose, contact her directly at theheartconnections@gmail.com.

References

American Heart Association "What Is Heart Failure?" *Https://Www.heart.org/* Retrieved from, www.heart.org/idc/groups/heart-public/@wcm/@hcm/documents/downloadable/ucm_30031 5

American Heart Association (2017, December 12) *Is Broken Heart Syndrome Real?* [Web log] Retrieved from http://www.heart.org/HEARTORG/Conditions/More/Ca rdiomyopathy/Is-Broken-Heart-Syndrome-Real_UCM_448547_Article.jsp#.WwbjcUgvzct

ESV Study Bible. English Standard Version, Bible Gateway, www.biblegateway.com/versions

Holy Bible. King James Version, Reference ed., Bible Gateway, www.biblegateway.com/versions

James A. Baldwin Quotes. (n.d.). BrainyQuote.com. Retrieved January 24, 2017, from BrainyQuote.com Web site: https://www.brainyquote.com/quotes/james_a_baldwin_1056 29

Johns Hopkins Medicine Health Library *Heart Transplant Surgery 101* Retrieved from https://www.hopkinsmedicine.org/healthlibrary/test_procedur es

Lundell, D. (2012, August 19) World Renowned Heart Surgeon Speaks Out on What Really Causes Heart Disease [Web log post] Retrieved from http://myscienceacademy.org

Mayo Foundation for Medical Education and Research (2017, December 23) *Heart Failure* Retrieved from http://www.mayoclinic.org/diseases-conditions

New International Version. Biblica, **1973**, **1978**, **1984**, 2011. Retrieved from www.biblegateway.com/versions/New-International-Version-NIV-Bible/

The Department of Cardiothoracic Surgery at the Montefiore-Einstein Heart Center NYC (2007, November 12) "Heart Transplant Procedure." Retrieved from youtu.be/cOBWMITf3co

UCLA Department of Molecular, Cell, and Developmental Biology *Molecular, Cell, and Developmental Biology* Retrieved January 10, 2018 from https://www.mcdb.ucla.edu/faculty/adeb

US Census Bureau (2016, November 17) *The Majority of Children Live with Two Parents, Census Bureau Reports* Retrieved November 21, 2017 from https://census.gov/newsroom/press-releases/2016/cb16-192.html

Zacharias, Ravi. (2017, January 29) "Living A Life Used By God|Nehemiah." Retrieved from YouTube. youtu.be/wVrvmDu7yMs.

Other Book by the Author

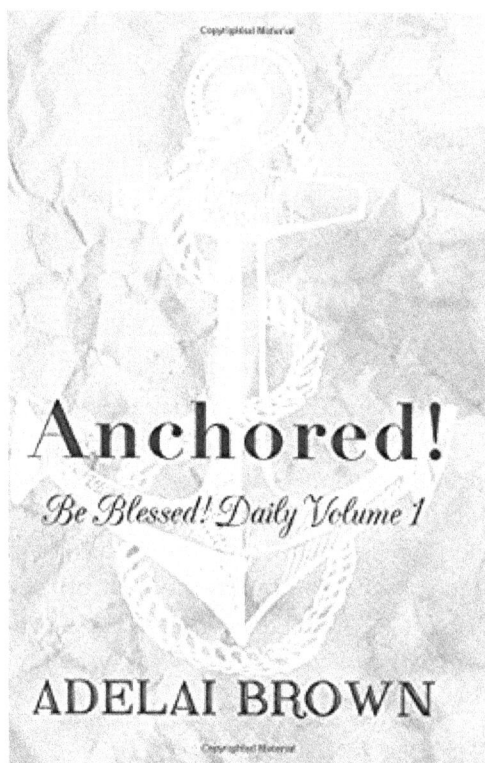

Anchored! is a daily devotional with 367 days of motivation and inspiration designed to anchor you during the winds, waves and trials of life. Whether motivating you to challenge yourself, trust in Jesus, or set your imagination free, these inspirational messages were ordained by God and have an uncanny way of reaching people at the right moment, wherever they are in their lives. Find reassurance, redirection, and instruction to stay anchored on your journey toward personal and spiritual growth.

http://bit.ly/anchoredvolumeone
ISBN-13: 978-1517524210
ISBN-10: 1517524210

Connect with Adelai

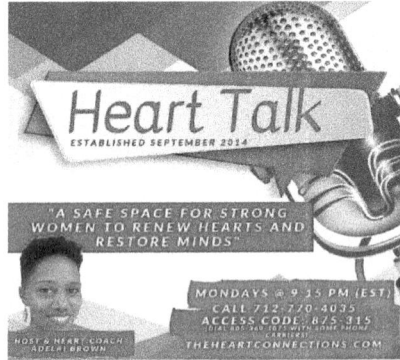

Ladies are invited to join Adelai every Monday night at 9:15 pm (EST) as she hosts, Heart Talk. Heart Talk is a women's empowerment session that is a safe space designed to help strong women renew their minds and restore their hearts. Established in September 2014, it has helped hundred of women (and some men) overcome their broken hearts.

Call 712-770-4035 access code: 875-315 to listen in LIVE.
For replay options call 712-770-4549 access code: 875-315

YouTube: @The Heart Connections
(bit.ly/heartconnections)

Facebook: @theheartconnections

Instagram: @theheartconnections

Twitter: @heartcoachtalk

Email: theheartconnections@gmail.com

www.ingramcontent.com/pod-product-compliance
Lightning Source LLC
Chambersburg PA
CBHW070054100426
42740CB00013B/2839